# History of the Maya

by Njord Kane

# History of the Maya

### By Njord Kane

Books may be purchased by contacting the publisher and author at: spangenhelm.com

Published on: March 1, 2016 by Spangenhelm Publishing

Interior Design and Cover by: Njord Kane

Library of Congress Control Number: 2015919659

ISBN-13: 978-1-943066-063

ISBN-10: 194306606-X

1. Maya  2. Mayan  3. History 4. Mesoamerica

First Edition.

10 9 8 7 6 5 4 3 2 1

**Spangenhelm Publishing**

United States

# Table of Contents

*For Jose' Luis and Kara Jo*

viii

# Preface

This book tells the Maya story chronologically from an anthropologist's point of view. Starting from the "First Peoples" that migrated into the Americas as hunter-gathers (the Paleo-Indians) following herds of megafauna, such as Mammoth. Into the gradual progression of settling and forming into a complex society.

The Maya were a major indigenous pre-Columbian civilization of the Yucatan Peninsula and are members of a modern American Indian people of southern Mexico, Guatemala, and parts of Honduras who are the descendants of this ancient civilization. [199] Which is correct to use when referring to these people, is it 'Maya' or is it 'Mayans?' Is it a 'Maya' or a 'Mayan' archaeological site? We see the words, Maya and Mayan used interchangeably without discrimination. So, which is correct, do we use Maya or Mayas or Mayan or Mayans?

The adjective 'Mayan' is used in reference to the

language or languages, whereas the noun "Maya"[**mah**-*yuh*][199] is used when referring to the people, places, and or culture, etc., without distinction between singular or plural. This convention is the most widespread among Mayanists (scholars who study and write about the Maya). This distinction arose in the field of linguistics, where the "Mayan" adjective started to be used to define the linguistic family that incorporates the different dialects spoken by the Maya people. In sum, "Mayan" are their languages and "Maya" for everything else in reference.

The purpose of this book is to provide a concise and up to date historical chronicle about the Maya. With so many recent discoveries by archeologists studying the Maya and their ruins, many things that we had previously knew of the Maya civilization have changed. This makes the Maya story as previously taught out of date and needing to be retold. This book tells the Maya story current to Today's discoveries, presented in short chapters to maintain the reader's enthusiasm through each epoch of Maya history.

We start our story about the Maya from first existence as an identifiable and distinct people that had migrated into the Americans many thousands of years ago. We will bring you to their progression from hunter-gathers into agricultural settlements that grew into city-states. A journey through the rise and decline of the Maya civilization.

This book is not the single work of the author, but the combined works of hundreds of years of thousands of researchers spending lifetimes trying to unravel the mystery of the Maya. There has been so many recent discoveries by modern researchers, the Maya story has almost been rewritten from what we thought we used to know about their obscure history.

# The Beginnings of a People

# Chapter 1

## Who were the Maya?

The Maya are an indigenous people whose culture had built a thriving ancient city-state civilization in Mesoamerica.

MesoAmerica is the location that lies in the area from Mexico to South America. An area considered to be the 'middle' of the Americas and is also known as the Central Americas.

Along with the Maya, there are many other indigenous cultures in the Mesoamerican area. Some of these other cultures are the Mexica (Aztecs), Mixtec, Purepecha, Huastec, Olmac, Toltec, Zapotec, and Teotihuacan.

These indigenous Mesoamerican cultures are credited with the creation and innovation of many inventions. They used advanced mathematics to engineer and build great pyramid temples that still stand after thousands of years. They were clear masters of observed astronomy and created highly accurate calendars. They maintained stable enough societies to allow the practicing of fine arts and integrated it into a complicated writing system that balanced both math and writing into a complex theology. The Maya are credited as being the first culture in the New World to utilize a fully developed written language.

They practiced elective medicine and for the most part, used an intensive agriculture system to maintain huge populations.

The Mesoamericans had discovered the wheel, but the absence of draft animals and an often demanding terrain made human labor the most utilized means for the transportation of goods and building materials. Suitable bovine or equine were not introduced into the Americas until later when Europeans brought them over.

M o

e k

x i Belize

Ho nduras

Guatemala

El
Salvador

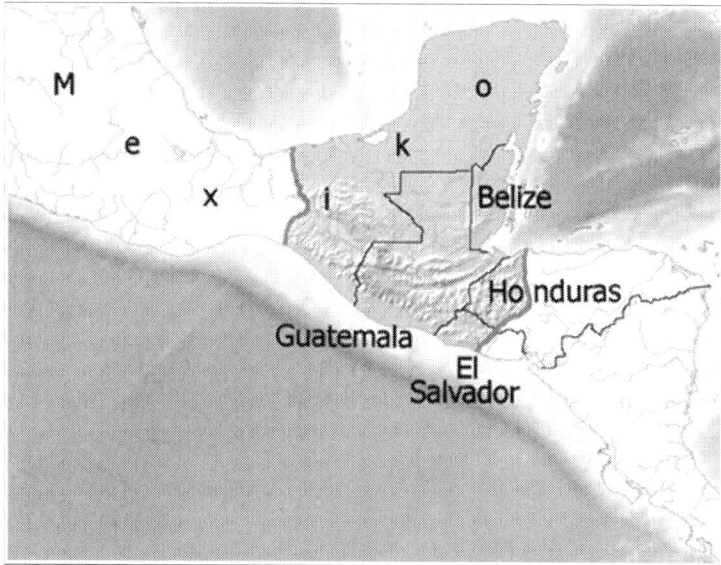

*Map showing the area where Ancient Maya were located in Mesoamerica.*[235]

The areas dominated by the Maya are known today as the southern Mexican states: Chiapas, Campeche, Yucatan, Quintana Roo, and Tabasco. The Maya civilization spread all the way through the nations of Guatemala, Belize, El Salvador, and Honduras.  A very large expanse of city-states that ruled the area linked by trade routes.

Descendants of the ancient Maya civilization live today in the Yucatán Peninsula of Southern Mexico, Guatemala, and parts of Honduras and El Salvador.

The proximity of the Mesoamerican people to each other in the region led to a high degree of cultural interaction between each other.  The consistent interaction between Mesoamerican civilizations within the region created a cultural diffusion that allowed Mesoamericans to share a great degree of their cultural practices and knowledge with each other.

Mesoamericans continually influenced each other, even when their interaction wasn't always peaceful. The writing and epigraphy used to create the famous 'Maya Calender' weren't even of Maya origination. They had assimilated it into their own culture from neighboring cultures in their region.

The writing used in the region had come from previous cultures and evolved over time within each different Mesoamerican culture. Script and usage becoming slightly altered or modified as each unique scribe used it in relation to their own culture.

The Maya people were not necessarily known as being great inventors themselves, but were instead great innovators that absorbed others advancements and continued to develop upon them within their own culture. The culture of the ancient Maya seemed to promote the application of inventions of the many other nearby cultures in the area and sought ways to improve upon them on their own.

Like many of the other Mesoamerican cultures, the Maya did not have a separation between religion and government. Church and State were one of the same. They considered the gods to be the everyday rulers of their daily lives and depended on their priests and rulers to ensure that the gods were appeased and didn't destroy the earth or extinguish the essential life sustaining Sun.

The Maya religion required a highly complicated method of worship that demanded bloodletting and sacrificial rituals that were often fulfilled by the kings and queens. These efforts were necessary because it was believed to "feed" the gods. It was the sacred duty and responsibility of the ruler to often feed the gods with their own blood. The believed their rulers had the power to pass in and out body to the spirit world and acted as messengers to the celestial world.[109]

Geographically, the Maya were formed individually as independent city-states. They used a government structure that allowed their individual rulers a great deal of individual governance within their own municipalities, instead of a strong centralized governing structure ruled by an emperor or empress.

The Maya civilization wasn't a single unified empire, but were instead a multitude of separate entities that shared a common cultural background. They shared several similarities with the Greeks, in that the Maya were religiously and culturally a nation, but were politically separate sovereign city-states.

*The center of Tikal, one of the most powerful Classic Period Maya cities.*[200]

Maya city centers were the epicenters for trade, religious, and other cultural activities which also included some local administration.[201] There were many Maya cultural centers located in what's considered "the Maya Area" that spreads across a large expanse covering a wide range of climate conditions. Their culture spanned across mountain ranges into semi-arid plains and reached into the thick labyrinths of the rain forests. A diverse area that allowed for a diversity of trade.

*Map of the Maya Area in the Yucatán peninsula.*[1]

The period of time before the arrival of Christopher Columbus and European expansion to the Americas is called the 'Pre-Columbian Period.' The Pre-Columbian period of Maya history divides into five distinct time periods.

- the Paleo-Indian Period ("First People" - 3500 BC),

- the Archaic Period (3500 BC - 2000 BC),

- the Preclassic Period (2000 BC - 200 AD),

- the Classic Period (200 AD - 900 AD),

- the Post Classic Period (900 AD - 1697 AD).

It was during the Paleo-Indian period when early nomads crossed into the Americas over 15,000 years ago. These were the "First People" to inhabit the Americas. They'd first crossed into North America until eventually splitting off from other groups and eventually migrating south through Mexico into the Yucatán Peninsula of Mesoamerica.

These migrating "First People" in the Maya region developed their tool and hunting technologies and went from being nomadic hunter-gatherers into forming more permanent settlements. These settled groups became more developed as they exploited the plentiful local resources.

These now settled groups progressed into the Archaic period and began advancing into a more complex society. These archaic settlements developed culture and technology that was shared with neighboring settled groups. The exchange of ideas between these groups formed into a shared culture that began developing into a culturally distinct people.

The Maya Civilization originated in the Yucatán region during the Preclassic Period at around 2000 BC. There is some argument as to when the Preclassic Period began for the Maya. It's argued to have began as late as 2600 BC, while there's claim that it's earlier because there are permanent Maya settlements along the Pacific coast that date to 1800 BC. A difference of eight hundred years, depending on region.

The Preclassic period begins where the first signs that the Maya can be recognized as a distinct people. The two time periods overlap each other as a result from different groups in the region gradually shifting from being a separate archaically developed people into adopting local culture and technology that was distinctly Maya.

It was also during the Preclassic period that the Maya developed a greater interest in art and began some degree of manufacturing. A number of Preclassic Maya pottery and clay figures that were fired in primitive kilns survive to this day. Many of these clay and pottery artifacts, that are well over four thousand years old, give us clues as to their origin and purpose. Indicators as to how advanced their technology was growing. The process of using buildings as a means of recording history had also began to develop during the Maya Preclassic era.

A very distinct Maya culture with religious beliefs and practices, as well as shared technologies, began to rapidly form and progress during the Preclassic period. Public ceremonies and rites begin taking place during the Preclassic period. The creation of burial rites for the dead began during this time. The Maya civilization continued to grow and advance into its Classical Period, where it reached its peak in development at around 200 - 250 AD. Still almost two thousand years before contact with Europeans.

The Classic Period for the Maya culture occurred from 200 to 900 AD. During this time, the Maya began to develop urban centers that were more focused on the pursuit of artistic and intellectual development. These city centers became true cultural hubs in various Maya city-states. Written documents from the Classical period demonstrate a highly developed method of communication amongst the Mesoamerican people. It was during the Classical period that engineering feats, such as the construction of pyramids in the city-states began emerging.

The desire to preserve personal and cultural histories begins to develop during the Classical period as well. There are many carved slabs of stone known as 'stelae' that have survived to tell the stories and lineage of important rulers of the time.

The Maya had developed a complex system of carved hieroglyphs to preserve the stories of historical events.

*Maya Stelae and Pyramid located at the Copan Ruins in Honduras.*[202]

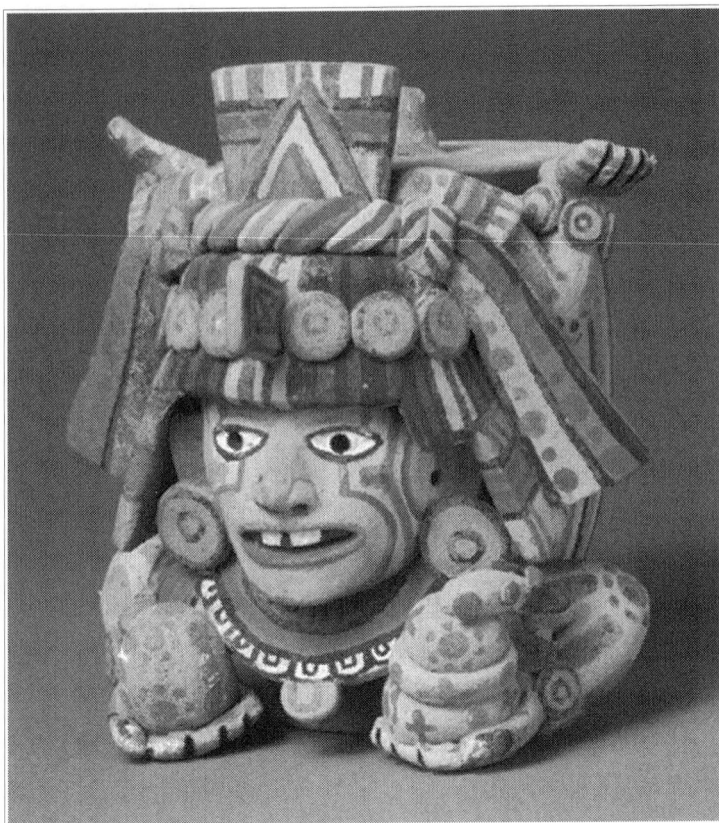

*Lidded effigy container in form of a god, Late-Postclassic period.*[213]

Towards the end of the Classic Period was when the structure of Maya society began to change. Settlements in the southern lowlands started dwindling in population until eventually becoming abandoned. This may be perhaps to natural disasters such as hurricanes known to the region. The architecture began appearing seemingly ordinary rather than having the elaborately ornate inscriptions that were apart of the buildings built centuries prior. Building took on a more utilitarian emphasis rather than the previous . There were few, if any, grand structures appearing in the 8th or 9th centuries leading into the Maya Post-classic Period.

During the Post-classic Period, the Maya people and their culture continued to thriving in the Northern sections of the Yucatan' area. Buildings in new settlements were now being constructed with plain straight walls and flat ceilings. These simple lines now characterized the construction of new buildings, in contrast to the elaborate carvings and decorations used in construction during the previous period.

The earlier interest in art continued to be part of Maya culture as well as a continued interest in language and writing, Yet the great bursts of creativity that came out during the earlier periods appear to have ceased during the Post-classic period of the Maya civilization.

Assimilation with other neighboring cultures had weakened some of the distinctiveness of Maya culture as they interacted more heavily on neighboring cultures. Nevertheless there were still several city-states that retained a decidedly distinctive Maya culture well into the 16th century.

During the Post-classic period the Maya civilization continued as a major dominating force for 700 more years until around 900 AD when their culture became less dominate in the region.

The Maya city-states continued through the arrival of the Spaniards in 1511 AD and continued until after almost two centuries of efforts by Spanish Conquistadors, the last Maya city was conquered in 1697 AD.

Even after the Spanish Conquest and subsequent colonization, the Maya people and the spoken Mayan language did not die out with the end of their civilization. The legacy of the Maya civilization lives on today in several ways. Many members of the rural populations in Chiapas, Guatemala, Belize, and the Yucatan Peninsula are Maya by descent and utilize one of the Mayan dialects as their primary verbal language.

The Culture of the Maya people can be found influencing many cultures around Mexico and other parts of Central America. Artifacts that are undeniably of Maya origin have been found as far away as Central Mexico, which is more than 1000 kilometers away.

# Chapter 2

# The Paleo-Indian Period

# (First People - 3500 BC)

In the history of Mesoamerica, the Paleo-Indian period applies specifically to when the very first indications of human habitation within the Mesoamerican region began. This is an event that took place during the stone age (paleolithic) stage of human evolution when migrating hunter-gatherers began permanently settling in areas.

The prefix "paleo" comes from the Greek adjective 'palaios' to describe something "old" or "ancient." The terms Paleo-Indian (Old Indian) or Paleo-Americans (Old Americans) refers specifically to the small bands of nomadic people whom first populated into the Americas during the final glacial episodes of the late Pleistocene period.

The Late Pleistocene period was when the final glacial episode of ice sheets covered much of the northern hemisphere. This event happened about 125,000 years ago and lasted until about 12,000 years ago.[237] Much of the Late Pleistocene age was dominated by glaciation. The land was taken over by towering sheets of ice such as the Wisconsin glaciation in North America and corresponding glacial periods in Europe and Asia. The towering glacial ice was impassable and reshaped the entire countryside.

## Extent of Late Pleistocene Glaciation in North America

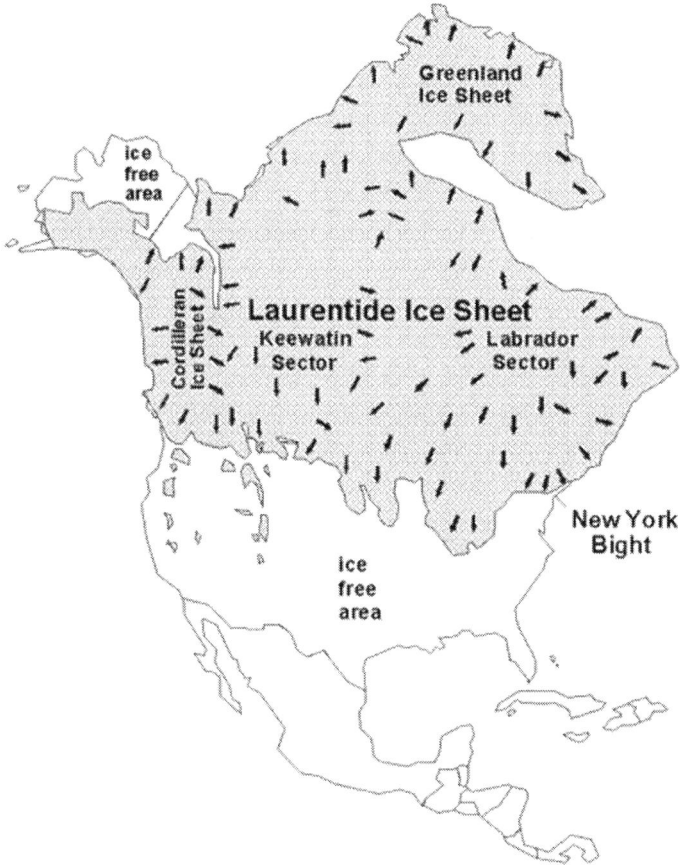

Greenland Ice Sheet

ice free area

Cordilleran Ice Sheet

**Laurentide Ice Sheet**

Keewatin Sector

Labrador Sector

New York Bight

ice free area

*North American map showing Late Pleistocene glaciation.*[236]

It wasn't until during the end of the Late Pleistocene period that the ice began to melt and the glaciers started to recede. It left land-ice bridges and these surviving human species were now able to cross and spread to every continent on Earth, except the Antarctica.

It was during the end of the Pleistocene period when the most recent episodes of global cooling from the last Ice Age took place. During this time much of the World's temperate zones were alternately covered by glaciers during cool periods and then uncovered during the warmer interglacial periods. During these warmer periods was when the glaciers retreated and allowed intercontinental passage.[110]

At the end of the last Ice Age, there were periods when sea levels lowered enough to create linking land and ice masses between Siberia and Alaska. These land-ice masses formed into what's called, "Beringia." The Beringia land-ice mass was about 580,000 square miles in range, which is roughly about twice the size of the state of Texas.

Beringia only existed when global sea levels fell enough to expose land masses that were joined together by ice. Beringia had existed during several periods in the Pleistocene time period.

During this time Beringia was connected to Siberia by a "bridge" made of land and ice. The Bering land-Ice bridge is believed to have existed both during the period glaciation that occurred more than 35,000 years ago and then again during a more recent period which lasted from 22,000 to 7,000 years ago. It was during the period between 16,000 to 12,500 years ago when the majority of humans crossed into the Americas from Siberia.[19]

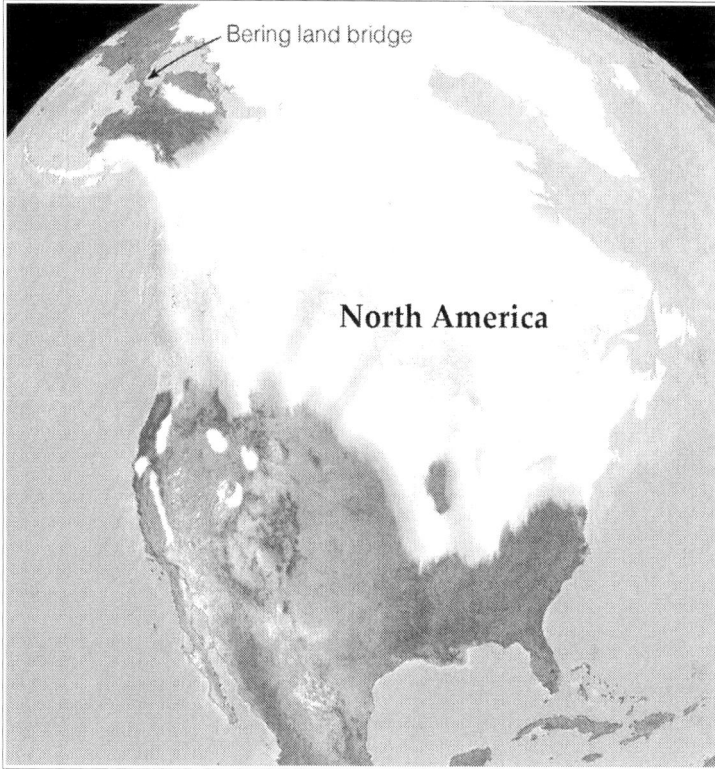

*Glacier Blocked Bering Land Bridge.*[206]

The Bering land bridge allowed passage between the two continents until sea levels began rising when the climate once again changed. Radiocarbon dating tests reveal that sea levels had lowered more than 400 feet below today's current levels from the growth of immense ice sheets in the Northern Hemisphere during the Ice Age.

The last warming, about 6000 years ago, is when the coastlines assumed their approximate sea levels and configurations that exist today.[215]

When the fifty-five mile long Beringia land-ice bridge was exposed, it was for a period the usually lasted approximately 3500 years.[205] Three to four millennia is more than a sufficient amount of time to allow wandering humans and other wildlife, such as mammoths, to cross into the Americas.

Based on plant life found from sea-core samples taken, it is believed that the area was covered with tundra plants and shrubs rather than being an arid grassland. This means that Beringia no longer provided adequate grazing for large herds of grazing animals.[205]

Some fauna and megafauna that crossed over were able to adapt and survive on what grazing and flora was available. But not all, many animals simply died off as a result of the lack adequate food sources. Many species were simply were hunted out of existence.

*Artist's depiction of Columbian Mammoths that roamed North America.* [238]

The big game hunters followed animals such as bison, mammoth, and mastodon through the Bering Strait from Siberia into North America when the Beringia land-ice bridge was exposed.[19][36]

These migrating hunters from Asia and Siberia became the Paleo-Indians to first occupy Beringia leading the way into North America.

*Paleo-Indians butchering a bison at the end of the Ice Age.* [214]

After they crossed over, rising sea levels and ice blocked their way back to Siberia. The land-ice bridge that allowed them to cross over was now gone. They couldn't return and glacial ice also blocked their passage further into the Americas. The first human entrants into the Americas had become trapped on Beringia for about 20,000 years.

Several generations had remained in Beringia until the ice receded to allow passage into the Americas.[208] During this period of time many megafauna had become extinct. Species of humans other than modern humans had either died out or were bred out during the Pleistocene glacial period.

The genetic traits that distinguish all Native Americans from non-native Americans had evolved during this twenty thousand year stay in Beringia. This period of isolation from other humans made a unique Native Americans. They are still similar to East Central Asians genetically, but have noticeable differences. Twenty thousand years is more than sufficient time to create the genetic polymorphisms that are distinguishably Native American.[208][209]210]

In many ways, indigenous Americans are linked to Asianics, specifically to eastern Siberian populations. The distribution of blood types and DNA link indigenous Americans to Asianics.[22] They are also linked by linguistic elements.

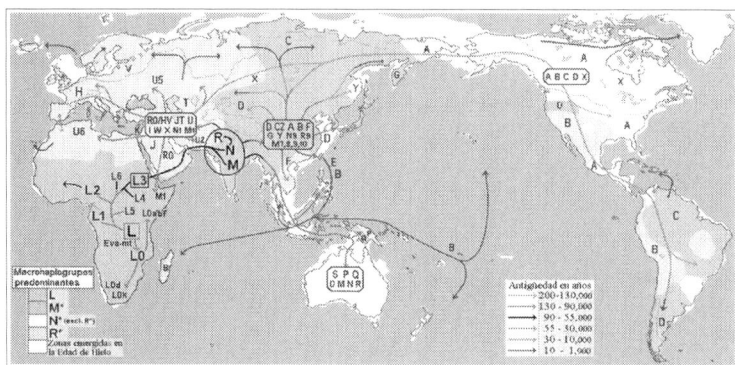

*Hypothesized map of human migration based on mitochondrial DNA.*[203]

After a long period of time the glaciers began to melt. The glaciers diminished rapidly enough that it could be seen over a person's lifetime. When the glaciers began melting and receding, the path into the New World opened. Beringia was no longer blocked by ice. However, the way back to Siberia was blocked by the sea. So the surviving humans and animals on Beringia migrated into the Americas.

Some of the earliest human settlements in North America were thousands of years before the latest glacial period when the land-ice bridge existed.[38] There were humans living in the northern parts of the Yukon area of Beringia when it was glacier-free 32,000 years ago.[39][40]

There were small groups of people that had passed through the Bering land-ice bridge as early as 40,000 years ago. Some of the first migrants to make it into the Americas. Most of the migration into the

25

Americas occurred 15,000 years ago. This was when migration through Beringia was simpler when the glacial ice had literally broken and opened large access paths into the Americas.

These new inhabitants were isolated groups of hunter-gathers that migrated alongside herds of large herbivores far into what is now known as Alaska.

About 18,500 to 15,500 years ago, ice-free corridors also developed along the Pacific coast and valleys of North America.[20] The warming climate began to transform the Beringia steppe into shrub tundra. This pushed the surviving megafauna and other wildlife to seek out better grazing lands.

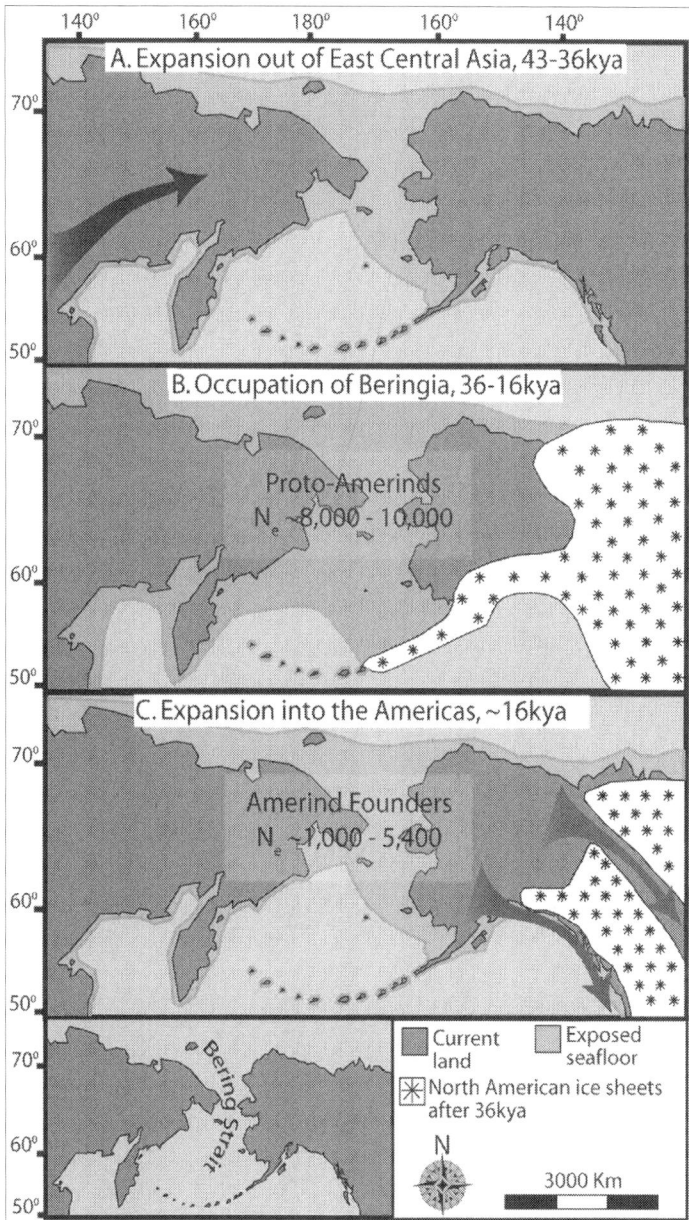

The phases of initial American migration by Paleo-Indians.[211]

The dwindling food sources also pushed the small isolated bands of Paleo-Indian hunter-gatherers into the New World. These hunting bands had followed herds of large herbivores through Alaska. When the ice free corridors developed, these large animal herds began migrating south through the Yukon Valley and made their way into the grasslands.

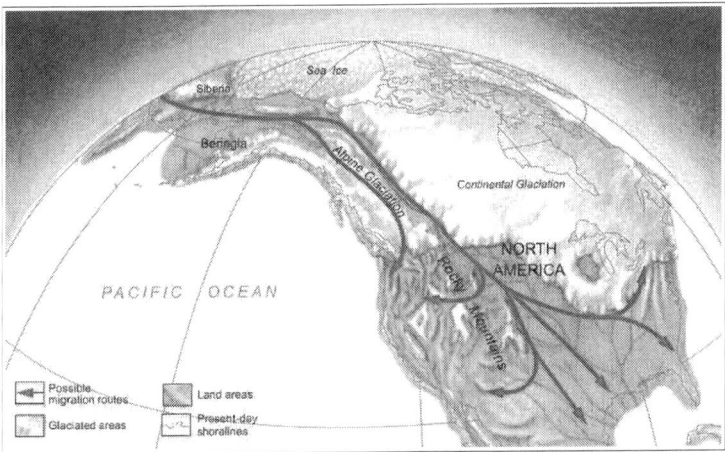

*Migration of Paleo-Indians.*[206]

Some groups continued migrating until they reached as far as the southern tip of South America. The new inhabitants had spread out into the Americas as far east as Virginia and past through the jungles of Brazil. They only stopped when the reached the oceans. Each group adapting to their new environments and evolving into their own distinct cultures.

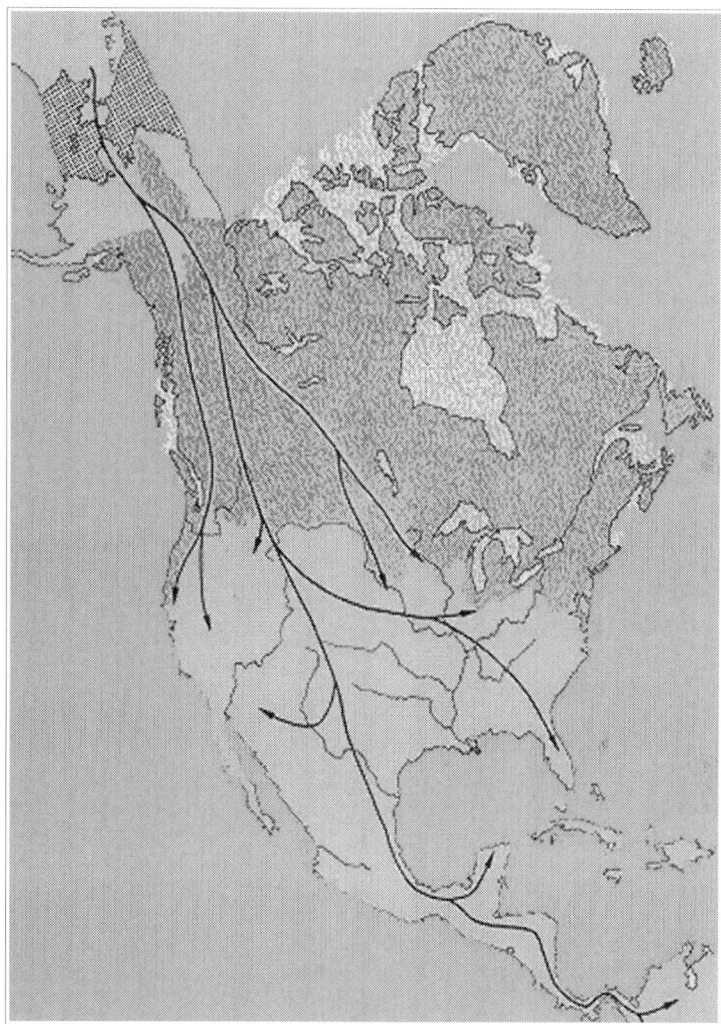

*Migration path of Paleo-Indians.*[207]

People from this period of time generally

concentrated on hunting various large game as their primary food source, but they also foraged for locally available foods.

The climate changes and competition for food sources would have caused longer migrations for some groups as they looked for consistent food sources. As the environment changed around them and the ice age ended, many animals migrated great distances seeking out new sources of food.[35]

*Paleo-Indians hunting a glytodont.*[23]

Some groups migrated along the Pacific coastal areas relying on fishing as their primary source of food.[37] With reliable food sources in some areas, many of these groups even permanently settled or at least stay in a certain range. Stone tools, projectile points and other artifacts that have been discovered give us evidence of the earliest human activity.

The types of artifacts, such as projectile points used with arrows and spears, tell us the approximate date and level of technology developed by early humans.

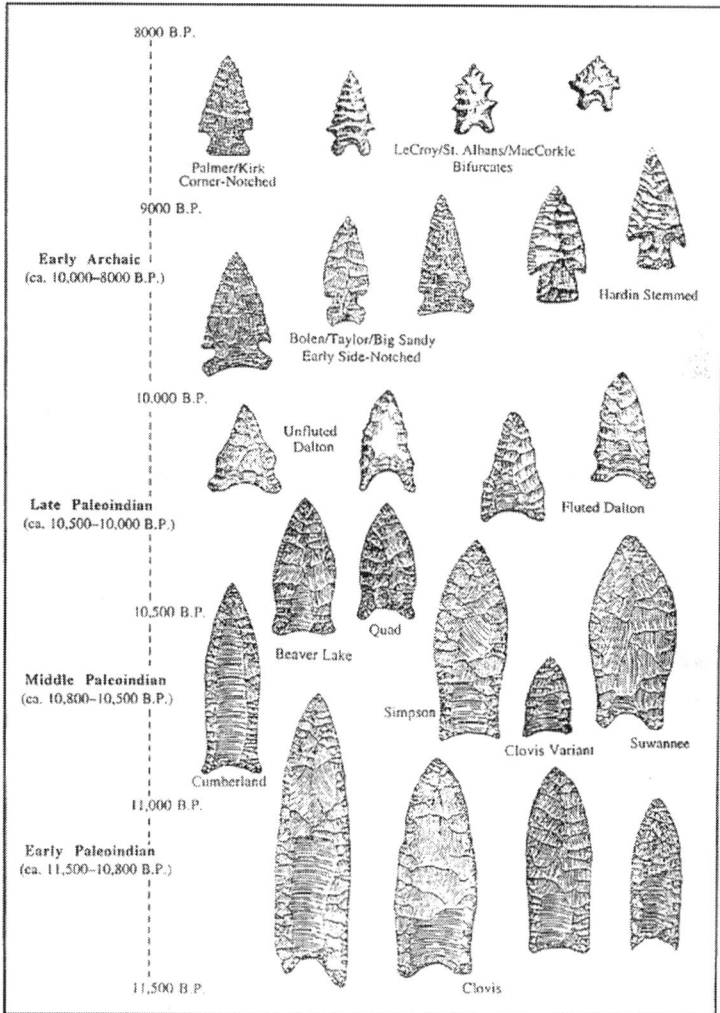

8000 B.P.

Palmer/Kirk
Corner-Notched

LeCroy/St. Albans/MacCorkle
Bifurcates

9000 B.P.

Early Archaic
(ca. 10,000–8000 B.P.)

Hardin Stemmed

Bolen/Taylor/Big Sandy
Early Side-Notched

10,000 B.P.

Unfluted
Dalton

Late Paleoindian
(ca. 10,500–10,000 B.P.)

Fluted Dalton

10,500 B.P.

Quad

Beaver Lake

Middle Paleoindian
(ca. 10,800–10,500 B.P.)

Simpson

Clovis Variant      Suwannee

Cumberland

11,000 B.P.

Early Paleoindian
(ca. 11,500–10,800 B.P.)

11,500 B.P.

Clovis

*Paleo-Indian Projectile Point Types.*[204]

31

Crafted stone age flaked tools (projectile points being the most commonly discovered) are used by researchers to classify the development of cultures and periods of use.[21]

Around 10,000 to 9000 years ago the climate stabilized and this led to a rise in population. Advances in Stone Age technology resulted in a more sedentary lifestyle. Humans began to settle in small groups populated by game and other stabilize food sources. The permanent peopling of the Americas had occurred by 9,200 BC.[24][25]

This time period in Mesoamerican history is referred to as the "Paleo-Indian period." This is the period when early human migration into the Mesoamerican region took place. A period of time that ranged roughly from 12,000 to 7000 years ago.

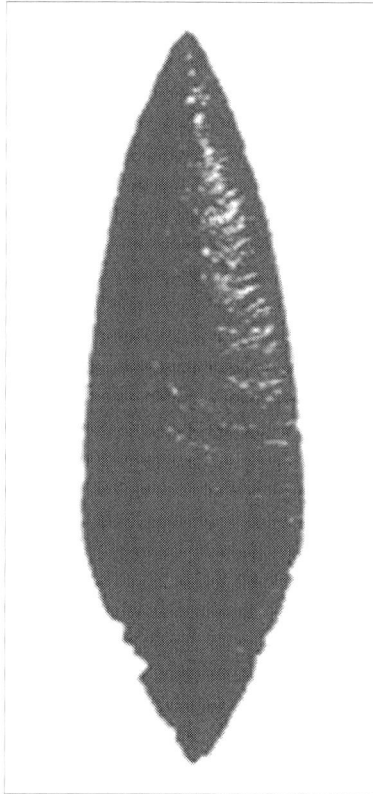

*Paleo-Indian obsidian projectile point from 9500 BC found in Guatemala.*[26]

Paleo-Indians are generally classified by their level of progression in stone age technology. The level of advancement in lithic or stone age technology used by these people is evaluated by the variety of techniques they used to produce various tools from stone. How advanced in the manufacturing and sophistication of tool making and types of tools they used.

Stone tools such as spear points and other projectile points would typically be made by chipping flakes from stone. Mesoamerican Paleo-Indians had the advantage of access to obsidian, which could be chipped into very sharp tools.

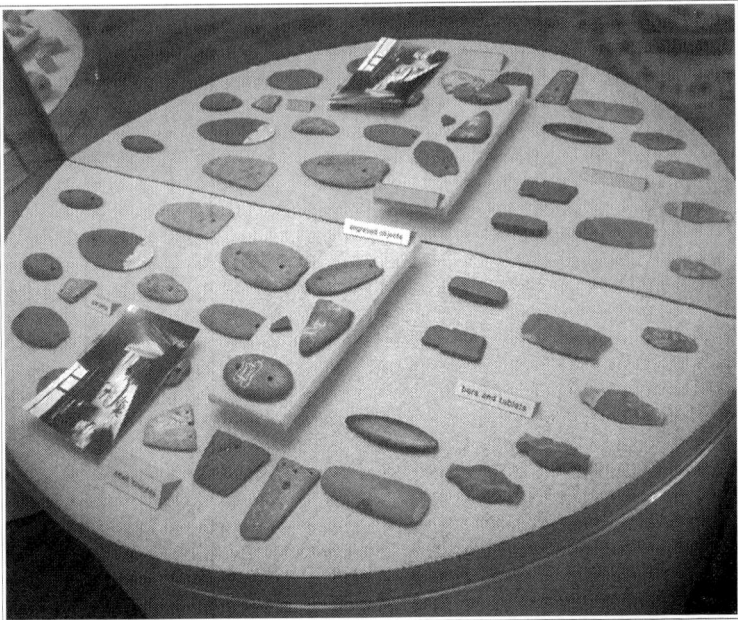

*Atlatl weights and carved stone gorgets from Poverty Point.*[31]

Fluted spear points were constructed from chipped stones with a long groove in the center added called a "flute." The fluted spear point was then tied on to the end of a spear or other projectile weapon. These weapon shafts were usually made from wood or bone.[32][33][34]

Man-made fluted points have been found in

northern Mesoamerica in the Mexican states of Sonora and Durango. The remains of a mammoth hunt have been discovered near Mexico City at Santa Isabel Iztapan and at Los Reyes la Paz.

Cranial discoveries also show early human presence in Mesoamerica during this period of time. In many locations, skulls have been found belonging to early Mesoamerican Paleo-Indians with remains of fauna and stone age artifacts made of obsidian. Discoveries showing evidence of a Paleo-Indian hunters, their prey, and the weapons and tools they used.

The Paleo-Indian time period lasts through until the onset of permanent settlements, agricultural development and other proto-civilization traits that lead into the Archaic time period in Mesoamerican history.

# Chapter 3

## The Archaic Period

## (3500 BC - 2000 BC)

The archaic stage was the second stage of cultural development in the Americas. The archaic stage is when most cultures began living more settled lives in contrast to continual migrating in search of food. They began improving their tools and used baskets for food gathering and storage. The beginning stages of agriculture come at this stage.

The period of time it took one culture to progress into this stage of cultural evolution varied from one group to another. Each culture's needs and availability to stable resources varied from one location to another.

This stage of development took place for most

cultures in the Americas anywhere from around 8000 BC to 2000 BC. Cultures that relied on fish and other stable local food sources were more likely to transition faster into this stage than others. Some groups continued to migrate and maintained a life of hunting and gathering to survive.

The Mesoamerican Archaic Period is characterized by subsistence economies that were supported through the regular exploitation of local food stuffs such as: nuts, seeds, and shellfish in addition to local hunting.

There are numerous different variations of these substance economies that have been identified. For example, the southwestern archaic cultures are subdivided into the Dieguito-Pinto, Oshara, Cochise and Chihuahua cultures.[217] They are subdivided because these cultures developed at different times and relied on slightly different regular food sources.

Dating a culture's progress is difficult at best and is highly dependent on rare finds. Archaic sites found in Northern Louisiana, Mississippi, and Florida show that many hunter-gatherer societies in the Lower Mississippi Valley region not only interacted with each other but traded and shared technologies. They had even organized together to build monumental mound complexes that date back as early as 3500 BC.

They continued to build these mound complexes for over half a millennium. Mound sites such as the ones found at Frenchman's Bend and Hedgepeth were of this time period and were all of localized societies.

The Watson Brake archaeological site in Ouachita Parish, Louisiana is considered to be the oldest mound complex in the entire Americas.[218] We can only speculate that these practices not only united some communities, but may have been the start of what would have eventually evolved into the Maya pyramid structures.

The Watson Blake site is nearly 2,000 years older than the site at Poverty Point, which is also located in Northern Louisiana. There are more than 100 regional sites associating with the Poverty Point culture of the Late Archaic period. These cultures regularly interacted with each other and had a regional trading network that connected to other cultures across the Southeast of North America.

Across the region of the Southeastern part of North America about 6,000 years ago, cultures were exploiting wetland resources and left behind large shell middens. These shell middens contained debris of human activity. Some of the shell middens discovered were processing areas where aquatic resources were processed directly after being harvested for use or stored in a distant location. Some shell middens were village dump sites. A treasure trove for archaeologists that get to collect information by items left behind or discarded by early archaic cultures.

Some middens found were directly associated with a house within a village. Each household would dump its garbage directly outside the house. These dump sites contain detailed records of what foods were processed and eaten. Often there would be fragments of stone tools and other household goods. Objects that are invaluable to archaeological studies.

Archaic period shell middens are numerous in the South Carolina and Georgia coastal regions. They're scattered around the Florida Peninsula and along the coast of the Gulf of Mexico. Resources were rich enough in these regions that it was able to support sizable mound-building communities all year-round.[219][220]

Archaic period sites across Mesoamerica resemble the same building methods and technology used by other groups spread throughout the Southwestern and Southeastern regions of North America.

*Artist's depiction of an Archaic period village.*[224]

Paleo and Archaic era groups carried influenced technologies from these groups with them as they migrated into the Mesoamerican region. These were the hunter-gather groups that were beginning to settle and merge into archaic settlements. These groups learned and developed near similar technological concepts and ideas within their own cultural practices. These cultural practices developed into being distinctively Mesoamerican.

The changed climate and an ever increasing human population with hunting techniques that continually improved, the large animals in the Americas began to perish. By 8,000 years ago, two-thirds of all North American animals weighing more than 100 pounds were now extinct. The Ancient Bison (bison antiquus) was the only large animal to survive on the vast ranges of the Great Plains.[221][222]

*Artist's depiction of an Archaic Camp Scene.*[223]

During the Archaic period a warmer and much more arid climate, in addition to excessive hunting, saw an end to the last megafauna in the Americas. Besides the bison, the great beasts that the first migrants for so long relied upon for sustenance were now gone.[27]

The majority of the population were in groups of highly mobile hunter-gatherers. But now some of these individual groups began to settle as they started to focus on resources available to them locally. As time passed these groups became permanently settled and shared knowledge, customs, and beliefs with neighboring groups.

These early settled groups progressed into the Basketmaker Era of the Archaic cultural period. This was when some groups became distinguishably different from other archaic settlements by the basketry they used to gather and store food.

These archaic basket weaving groups became reliant on wild seeds, grasses, nuts and fruit for food. Often they'd changed their movement patterns and lifestyle in order to maximize gathering the edible wild food and small game within a geographical region.

With the extinction of megafauna, hunters had adapted their tools and began using spears with smaller projectile points. They began using the atlatl and darts for smaller game. Shelters and other simple dwellings were made out of wood, brush and earth. The entirety of their lifestyle changed as they improved upon adapting to their settled environments.

Many archaic groups progressed into planting and using agricultural crops. Typically they grew maize, beans, and squash. Their agricultural methods gradually improved over time as their settlements grew larger and agriculture became a more reliable and important source of subsistence.[78]

There was still an absence in these archaic cultures of any formal social stratification. There isn't any form of writing or any major architecture structures being built beyond mound building.

Agriculture continued to develop as permanent villages established themselves in the region. Later in this period the use of pottery and loom weaving became common. Societal class divisions also began to appear in some settlements. The late archaic period is when basic technologies in terms of stone-grinding, drilling, and pottery were established in Mesoamerica.

Regional adaptations to common skills and technologies became the norm during the late archaic time period. Many groups continued as game hunters, but their hunting methods became more sophisticated. Other methods of procuring food became more complex as well.

Most groups became less reliant on traditional hunting and gathering practices. They now had growing mixed economies of small game, fish, seasonally gathered wild vegetables and other harvested foods. Harvesting food to trade with other settled groups for other food stuffs was now common.[28][29][30]

A culture's progression out of the archaic stage is defined by their adoption of sedentary farming. This progression varied significantly across the Americas; but by 2000 BC, the majority of Mesoamerican cultures had made their transition out of the archaic stage.[216]

# Chapter 4

## Preclassic Maya (2000 BC – 200 AD)

The Maya Preclassic period is divided into three time periods: the Early Preclassic, the Middle Preclassic, and the Late Preclassic period. The Preclassic Period of Maya history begins where the first settlements have evidence of crop cultivation. This period began from around 2000 BC to 2600 BC and lasted until around 200 AD to 250AD.

Most Maya groups had already transitioned out of the archaic period and were already becoming distinguishably Preclassic Maya. Their cultural practices which were now unique to their people and they had built agricultural based settlements.

The earliest Maya came into the tropical lowland areas around modern day Belize as farmers before the Preclassic period over 4,000 years ago. These ancient Maya started building their storied cities in MesoAmerica as early as 1000 BC.[276]

The Early Preclassic Period marks the beginnings of agriculture. These are the settled groups that slowly grew into settlements that improved upon their knowledge of growing foods. Their settlements grew in size because of reliable agricultural methods that were able to provide sustenance for their growing populations.

*Some sample varieties of maize cultivated by the Maya.[245]*

Knowledge of maize use and cultivation was passed on from one group to another throughout the Southwestern portion of North America. This agricultural knowledge was carried into Mesoamerica by migrating farmers whom brought their learned farming methods with them. The knowledge was gradually shared through interaction between other groups. [245]

There are differences in cultivation techniques used by different groups and even different words used for maize. These differences in cultivation methods and terminology tell us that their methods developed after these groups had already settled into early organized societies. Their maize culture differed from that of other groups across the Americas.

The time it took some Mesoamerican groups to transition into an agricultural culture stretched over a period of nearly two thousand years. The abundance of local foods that was readily available made cultivation and general agriculture something that was adopted slowly. Most of their dietary proteins were obtained primarily from the meat of local game. There was no great need to adopt agriculture until growing populations demanded it.

The earliest regular planned cultivation of maize in the Maya area dates before the Preclassic period. In Guatemala, evidence of early field burning has been found that dates before 2000 BC. These field burnings were most likely done annually, which is a practice used to ready crop fields for the following Spring.

There is pottery and architecture that date from 2000 BC to 1000 BC associated with this phase of Preclassic culture. In Belize, this kind of field burning agriculture and other soil manipulation methods had been used by early preclassical Maya. Additionally ceramic items have been found in these site locations that also date to the Preclassic period.

The early preclassic era Maya agriculturalists in Belize had grown domesticated maize, fruits, cacao and a variety of root crops. Yet their diet was only partly supplied by these domesticated crops. There was still a high dependence on the readily available foods that could be acquired locally through hunting, fishing, and plant foraging. These food sources were an important part of the first Maya's diet. Social organization was predominately family-centered and based on subsistence.

The Middle Preclassic period was between 1000 BC and 300 BC. There are numerous Middle Preclassic settlement sites across most of the Maya area that easily date archaeologically to this period. During this time, the Maya ultimately spread into the interior areas when many moved up the river valleys from the coast. Hurricanes most probably being the main motivator for moving inland.

Communities were still small and sites discovered where they built houses were wide spread. The more significant communities in the Middle Preclassic period were in the interior regions which became the heartland of the Maya civilization. These were the communities that later became prominently developed with public architecture built during the Classic Period.

Public architecture began being built in these settlements when their populations grew significantly larger, such as the sites found in Cuello, Cerros, Nohmul, and Lamanai in northern Belize.

The Belize River Valley area had scattered houses with public platforms in their local centers. Middle Preclassic period buildings have also been found in Cahal Pech, Pacbitun and at El Pilar.

From 300 BC to 250 AD during the late preclassic period, the lowland Maya population continued to expand which resulted in greater competition for land and resources. This competition led to increased population densities in the larger Maya settlements and surrounding areas.

It became necessary to develop better resource and agricultural management strategies. The Maya began developing more complex and elaborate ways for coordinating, organizing, and feeding their growing populations.

This required the establishment of leadership in the form of Maya aristocracy with its corresponding societal hierarchy. This new ruling institution and its dynasties would shape the history of the Maya people through the Postclassic Period.

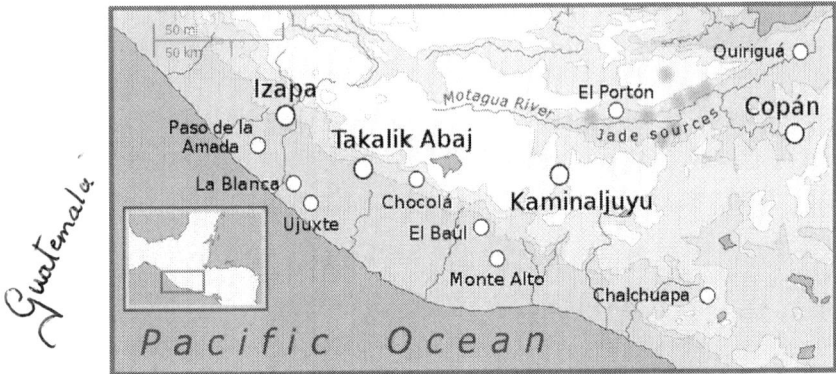

*Preclassic sites in the lower Maya area.*[246]

Many settlements gradually grew into major Maya city-states such as the ones in Izapa, Copan, Kaminaljuyu and El Mirador. Many of these city-states grew to being very prominent and powerful. Influencing their surrounding settlements and ruling families of different city-states often conducted warfare against each other.

The city-state of El Mirador grew to prominence and united with other states in the Maya lowlands. El Mirador dominated the lowlands until its decline and the city was eventually abandoned somewhere around 100 to 300 AD.

It's possible that the rulers of El Mirador became the Kaan Dynasty of Calakmul[2] Rivaling the city-state of Tikal in power and influence, Calakmul would become one of the two dominate powers of the Preclassical Maya era.

*The Lost City of the Maya, El Mirador.*[247]

Calakmul was one of the largest and most powerful of the ancient preclassic maya city-states. Calakmul is the city-state's modern name, in preclassic times it was known as "Ox Te' Tuun."

Calakmul was a major Maya power within the northern Yucatan region of southern Mexico. The dynasty of Calakmul administered over a large domain known as the Kingdom of the Snake. The snake head sign, which read as "Kaan." The emblem

53

glyph of the Snake Kingdom was marked everywhere within their domain.[79]

A fragmented block at El Palmar represents an emblem glyph of Kaan, the Snake Dynasty of Calakmul.[80]

The Late Preclassic Period was one of major activity and cultural change. The population in the interior around the city-state of Tikal, modern day Guatemala, was dense since its rise to dominance. The Maya were also already engaged in early monument building projects at this time. There were considerable public constructions at major locations at Tikal and other interior centers. They used their newly merged surrounding communities to consolidate power and expand their influence.

The city-states of Nohmul, Lamanai, El Pilar and

Cerros also grew to their peaks of power. They commanded the loyalty of large domains that contained many well established settlements and were firmly rooted by end of the preclassic period. Major public constructions of platforms and pyramids are found throughout different sites of these great preclassic era city-states.

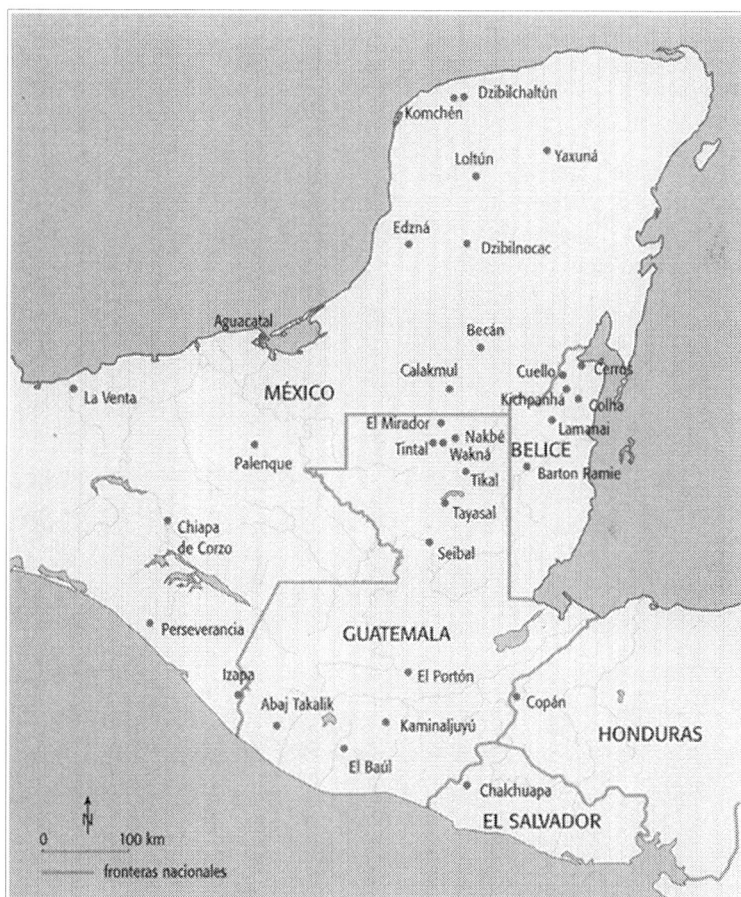

Map of Preclassic Maya sites.[248]

# Chapter 5

## Early Preclassic (2000 BC - 1000 BC)

The Early Preclassic Era is the time period when the beginnings of agriculture emerge in Maya culture. The earliest evidence of agricultural field burning and cultivation of maize along with other crops dates well before the beginning of the Early Preclassic period. Agriculture was already being practiced in some areas of Guatemala that were settled by distinctively Maya groups.

The very roots of Maya civilization are obscure at best. However as our understanding of new and old discoveries increases, we're more able to paint a vague picture of their early beginnings. By around 2000 BC, the southern Maya area had already been occupied by early speakers of Mayan languages. We know that this area was occupied by archaic Maya groups prior to the early preclassic era. The first more permanent settlements were already beginning.

It was during the early preclassic period when the Maya culture transitioned from hunter-gatherers into agricultural based communities. They'd began experimenting with cultivating a variety of food bearing and edible plants. These grown crops were already become a major component of Maya diet. They grew a selection of root crops, domesticated maize and fruits. Cacao had not only made it into their diet but also was sometimes used as a form of currency.

But even with the presence of agriculture, grown crops still only made up for less than 30% of their diet. Fish, meat from hunting and other gathered foods still made up for the majority of their diet.[3] During the early preclassic period, the Maya at Cuello subsisted primarily on shell fish, deer and several small mammals in the local area. They supplemented their diet with corn, beans, squash and a variety of other plant foods. So even though these Maya settlements had transitioned into early preclassical agriculture, they retained a degree of their archaic hunter-gathering practices.

When agriculture gradually began to develop, so

did the appearance of basic pottery. The Maya developed early pottery in simple design using a type of ceramics called "swasey." This type of pottery is relatively simple in form and predominantly reddish in color. These types of ceramic artifacts are what help us date these settlements specifically to the early preclassic era.

North of the progressing Maya, in the area of modern day Tabasco, Mexico, the Olmec culture was advancing. The presence of these Olmecs would have a profound impact on Maya society and culture. The early Maya began trading and interacting with the more advanced Olmec over a prolonged period. This contact altered the Maya way of life in almost every aspect.

The Olmecs were the first significant civilization to develop in Mesoamerica. They are essentially the mother culture of pre-Hispanic Mexico. The Olmec people were also known by other groups as the "rubber people."

Their religious beliefs venerated the jaguar as a supernatural being. There are Olmec artifacts which bear the images of the were-jaguar. The were-jaguar combined the physical characteristics of both humans and felines. These artifacts have been found scattered in several locations throughout Mexico. The were-jaguar artifacts show just how far the influential reach of Olmec culture was in Mesoamerica. Various Olmec-like symbols that were carved and painted on their relatively more sophisticated pottery have been found half way up the Mexican Gulf coast in the state of Veracruz.

In the lowlands near the Gulf Coast of the Mexican states of Veracruz and Tabasco are remains of Olmec ceremonial centers. An important Olmec political and religious center that flourished between 1200 and 900 BC is located in the Coatzacoalcos River basin of San Lorenzo.

The Olmec had also built the first conduit drainage system known in the Americas. An amazing advancement in engineering, but the Olmec are best known for the six colossal basalt heads. These massive stone heads are eight to nine feet in height and weigh from twenty to forty tons each.

These colossal heads were carved from stone that were obtained more than 50 miles away and were brought to the site. A monolithic undertaking for a post stone age / early agricultural people. These stone monolith faces have noticeably negroid facial features, even though they are uniquely Olmec in origin.

*Olmec Colossal Head 3 in San Lorenzo.* [239]

The Colossal Heads also appear to be wearing helmets, something that has puzzled researchers ever since they were discovered. The first Olmec head was discovered at Tres Zapotes where at the same time 'Stelae C' was discovered. Markings on Stelae C bear the Olmec calendar long count date which converts to 31 BC. This date on the stelae gives us a probable date for the placement of the Colossal Head.

More gigantic heads like the one at Tres Zapotes, in addition to a number of massive stone altars and stelae, have been discovered at the La Venta site. This site was the Olmec people's most important cultural center. It was their capital city, the cultural

61

heart of their society. These massive stone works were somehow floated by means of using waterways to La Venta. The La Venta site is located on an island near the Gulf Coast in the present-day Mexican state of Tabasco.

The Olmec center at La Venta shares essential characteristics with all Mesoamerican centers later built by different cultures in the area. The site is laid out along a north and south axis with a huge earth and clay pyramid as its most prominent feature.

The Olmecs were a very advanced culture for their time. They were the first Mesoamerican people to understand the concept of zero, which is essential in mathematics. They were the first to develop a calendar and were the first to create an hieroglyphic writing system to record events. The Olmec's intellectual achievements, religious beliefs and rituals were very influential on the neighboring cultures around them. Cultures such as the Maya, Zapotec, Mixtec and Aztec were all heavily influenced by Olmec culture.

Many Mesoamerican communities appear to have been permanently occupied prior to 1200 BC. It is within this period of the early preclassic period that the earliest Maya villages were found to be occupied in northern Belize. The settlement in Cuello was also settled by Maya around 1200 BC.

This was a time in when the heavily Olmec influenced Maya began to come together as a city builders.

Their early settlements were now being built with a greater sense of permanence. The early settlement inhabitants even erected their thatch houses on low apsidal shaped (oval) platforms. These platforms were constructed using a lime-gravel mixture called sascab, in addition to using white lime and stone.

Although most of the structures in their settlements were residential homes, but a few structures were built as shrines specifically where important rituals were conducted by members of the community. Religion in the form of Mesoamerican blood rituals was now firmly a part of Maya culture. One structure found at the Cuello site had contained more than 20 skeletal remains of individuals whom may have been sacrificed to commemorate the construction of the community's holy shrine.

The first Maya settlers in Cayo also appear to have also moved into the area at around 1200 BC as had other Maya. They established their settlements on the hills along the major river systems. They built communities on the hilltop where they farmed the rich alluvial valleys, also collecting jute and hunted wild game. Like the colonizers of Cuello, the early Maya in the Belize River Valley constructed large and small apsidal shaped platforms on which they built wattle and daub buildings with thatched roofs.

Maya buildings weren't without decoration, we've learned from fragments of preserved stucco at the Cahal Pech site that the plaster walls of these buildings were painted in red and white bands.

Their populations began to grow as their settlements grew with them. Broad cultural changes and increases in urban activity in Mesoamerica because corn began providing enough calories to trigger a move to a more settled and urban existence. [278] The spread in population demanded denser city building as available real estate became more and more scarce. The ancient Maya started building their storied cities as early as 1000 BC.[278]

This was the beginning of what later became the well known tall Maya cities with their steep pyramids and ceremonial platforms.

*1000 BC Ceremonial platform at Ceibal Guatemala.*[279]

A ceremonial platform built at Ceibal, Guatemala that dates to around 1000 BC, appears to precede the pyramid and plazas built in the Olmec city of La Venta in Tabasco, Mexico, at around 800 BC. The Olmec center at La Venta appears to have been deliberately destroyed sometime around 400 to 300 BC. There has not been any discoveries of why, but speculation points to conquest by a neighboring culture that conquered and destroyed the Olmec along with their civilization.

Numerous other Maya sites and related ones on the Pacific Coast show signs of growing from settlements into cities with ceremonial centers at around 1000 BC. The date from 1200 to 1000 BC appears to be the period of time when most Maya settlements progressed into the early preclassic period and built either cities or large settlements. Their interaction with each other and other cultures helped to progress this.

The Early Preclassic Maya had regularly traded and exchanged goods with both local and distant people. They were able to import obsidian, jade and iron pyrite from different regions in Mesoamerica. They even acquired conch shells for jewelry and salted reef fish from the Caribbean coast. This trade and regular interaction between other cultures and other Maya settlements helped push their knowledge and technology ever further as they progressed into the middle preclassic period.

# Chapter 6

## Middle Preclassic (1000 BC - 400 BC)

The Maya middle preclassic period began around 1000 BC. During this same time in other parts of the World, David becomes king of the ancient Israelites and the Iron Age begins for much of Eurasia. Across the Pacific ocean, the ancient Japanese begin to cultivate rice. Everywhere in the World cultures were thriving.

This was the period of time when the roots of a complex Maya society began to steadily form and they became a more advanced people. A progression that occurred after centuries of agricultural village life and trade. Food abundance allowed for leisure time which allowed time for innovation and invention. Their settlements grew into cities and as their needs changed they built accordingly.

They were now building canals and irrigation systems that demanded planning and coordinated human effort. The organized use of manpower began to appear with increasing complexity and scale. Society changed and social classes formed.

Prestige items such as obsidian mirrors and jade mosaics began to appear, demanding a more extensive trade network that reached well past the boundaries of the Maya civilization. Social classes and privilege now existed within the kingdoms. The nobility made sure to firmly secure their position of privilege with the help of priests working to appease their gods and pacify the people.

A nobility structured religious culture had transformed the Maya into a ritualistic centered society. Central plazas and earthen mounds gradually began to be included in villages. Desperate to appease their gods, on occasion some of these religious structures would be enhanced by masonry.

A mound in La Blanca, Guatemala is more than 75 feet tall and contains a fragment of masonry that strongly resembles an Olmec style carving of a head. The neighboring Olmec culture had a profoundly strong influence on Maya Culture. Maya began to carve stone stelae during this period of the preclassic era. They adorned the stelae with portraits of rulers, but the carvings were still devoid of any kind of writing yet.

The stelae in the city-state of Copan in western Honduras mark royal dynasties of the kingdom. The site was known for its development in agriculture long before stone architecture began being built there in the 9th century BC. The Copan river valley was rich and fertile and the Maya of that region thrived. The bounty from the land was plentiful and able to support artisans to produce sculptures and other carvings.

*Maya Stela, at Copan, Honduras*[13]

Early sculptors used a variety of media, including stone, wood, stucco and clay. Unfortunately, many of these works of that were created with perishable materials have deteriorated and are rarely found by archaeologists.[4][5]  There is an abundance of cultural information about the middle preclassic Maya that will forever be lost in time.

In the southeastern region of the Maya area at around 900 BC, the La Blanc city-state dominated the Pacific coastal region to around 600 BC when the kingdom's rule collapsed.  This 300 year reign of the La Blanc Maya is called the Conchas phase. The Conchas phase's progression is measured by their changes in pottery.

Changes in ceramics give us an idea of their level of technological progress, such as the introduction of fine paste ceramics.  There were few imported ceramics in the region.  Those that were imported were few and less decorative.  Most of the ceramics were produced locally.

*Middle preclassic Maya pottery.*

Religion appears to have been a dominate factor

in preclassical Mesoamerican life, not just for the Maya but for all the surrounding cultures as well. One of the first temples in Mesoamerica had been built at around 900 BC. This temple was 150 x 90 meters at its base and stood over 25 meters tall.[6] A colossal structure that took planned engineering and coordinated man power to be built solely on the basis of religion.

Besides building massive structures such as temples, there has been various other types of religious paraphernalia found in household dig sites. Figurines are the most numerous items of religious paraphernalia found at many of the Preclassic Mesoamerican sites.

*Ceramic seated male figurine and a female figurine, both of 600-900 AD.*[14]

Many archaeologists and other researchers interpret the discovered figurines as being religious artifacts that were used in domestic rituals, Figurines such as these are especially used for ancestral veneration. ancestral veneration was a practice most probably carried over from Siberia from early Paleo-Indians, as it was commonly practiced throughout the Americas is a variety of forms. Besides appeasing household gods and venerating ancestors, figurines were also used to mark important milestones in the life-history of individuals. Especially that of important figures and rulers.[7][8][9][10][11]

Agriculture, architecture, and religion weren't the only things that dominated Maya life, warfare appears to have intensified during the middle preclassic period. Maya weaponry starts becoming more advanced. Maya rulers begin to be portrayed as warriors and heroes. Additionally, the appearance of mass graves and decapitated skeletons found belonging to this period are undeniable of evidence of battles.

The Maya did not maintain large standing armies as did the Greeks, Egyptians, or the Romans. Instead, they conscripted able-bodied men and boys to muster together a militia. These mustered militias would then be armed from centralized arsenals kept in public buildings. Usually they were armed with stone clubs, spears and fire hardened wooden axes with flint or obsidian blades on the edges.

Besides melee weapons, they were also armed with blowguns, javelins and other projectile weapons such as slings, bows and arrows, and Atlatl spear throwers. Maya soldiers typically carried long, flexible shields of hide or smaller rigid round shields, but this wasn't always the case for mustered militia as it was for private soldiers and personal guards of nobility and the elite.

*Maya warrior from set of History Channel's*
*"Warriors: Maya Armageddon."*[84]

Many warriors wore body armor that was made
from cotton vests that were stuffed with rock salt.
This armor was so effective that hundreds of years
later, Spanish conquistadors would shed their own

metal armor in the sweltering rain forest in favor of these Maya salt rock filled cotton 'flak jackets.'

The Maya also had a war helmet made of pyrite stone called a "Kohaw." These unique helmets were only wore by special soldiers such as the Ajaws (or Ahau meaning 'Lord,' usually a nobility title) and Kaloontes (meaning supreme warrior or military ruler). An example of these 'Kohaw' helmets were found inside a queen's tomb in the El Perú site, also known as the 'Wak,' in northern Guatemala.

*El Perú 14.8 cm clay figure with removable Kohaw helmet.*[94]

The queen's tomb was uncovered at a site in the ancient Maya city-state of El Perú, which was the capital of the Wak Kingdom. It is believed that the queen's tomb belonged to none other than Lady K'abel whom was a military ruler of the Wak, or 'Centipede Kingdom,' between the years 672 to 692 AD.

The tomb was found in the ruins of the ancient

city's main pyramid temple. Maya hieroglyphs in the tomb include the names: "Lady Water Lily Hand" and "Lady Snake Lord." Both of these names are thought to refer to Lady K'abel, whom had governed the Wak kingdom for her family, the Kan. The Kan dynasty is better known as the Snake dynasty. The Snake dynasty was based in the Maya capital of Calakmul, located in what's now Mexico.

Even though Lady K'abel ruled with her husband, K'inich Bahlam, she held the prestigious title of Kaloonte, meaning 'supreme warrior.' This title gave her a higher authority than even her husband, the king.

Like many Noble families worldwide, the Snake dynasty had a policy of marrying off its princesses and noblewomen to the kings of vassal states like that of the Wak Kingdom to the Kan Dynasty. These royal unions were not only to consolidate power, but were also in favor of achieving a greater unity in the southern Maya Areas. To control the southern Maya region was also controlling the rich breadbasket area that also contained the coveted cacao bean.[76]

The cacao bean has been an extraordinary and intensively cultivated commodity of enormous importance in Mesoamerica. The Maya used cacao in their cuisine, religion and even used it as currency. It was a commodity of high value and importance to

Mesoamericans everywhere.

Cacao was so coveted that there are actually carved stone sculptures and figurines from the southern Maya area in Guatemala that depict decapitation and other sacrifices performed that were associated with cacao. These stone sculptures representative the fierce warfare that was waged over this commodity. Hundreds of years later, Spanish Conquistadors would make reference to Mesoamerican natives always fighting over the production and distribution of the cocoa bean and its various processed forms.[77]

The Maya called cacao, "kakaw" and like most Mesoamericans, believed that it was the food of the gods. They boiled the cacao bean and then mixed it with various peppers and spices to make a drink out of it.

Christian nuns on missionary in Mesoamerica believed that the diabolical powers of chocolate were due to the chili peppers and spices, so they replaced them with vanilla, sugar and cream with delightful results. So delightful, that the nuns would spend all day making chocolate and not tend to their missionary duties and had to be forbade from making it.

# Chapter 7

## Late Preclassic (400 BC - 200 AD)

During the Late Preclassic period, populations throughout the Maya area continued to increase. Many new settlements were founded and they quickly grew in size. Settlements that had been established during the Middle Preclassic period, continued developing and grew even larger.

The Late Preclassic period saw the rise of two powerful states that rivaled each other in scale and monumental architecture later in the Classic period. These were the Maya city-states of Kaminaljuyu in the highlands and El Mirador in the lowlands.

There were many important city centers that laid along trade routes that interconnected the Maya. Trade reached from the highlands all the way to the coastal regions of Mesoamerica. This increased trade fostered contact with other communities and brought in new ideas that were constantly being exchanged from region to region.

It was during the Late Preclassic period that all the major achievements of ancient Maya civilization were in place. An extensive trade network allowed the regular exchange of ideas and the people of preclassic period were already developing as a complex culture.

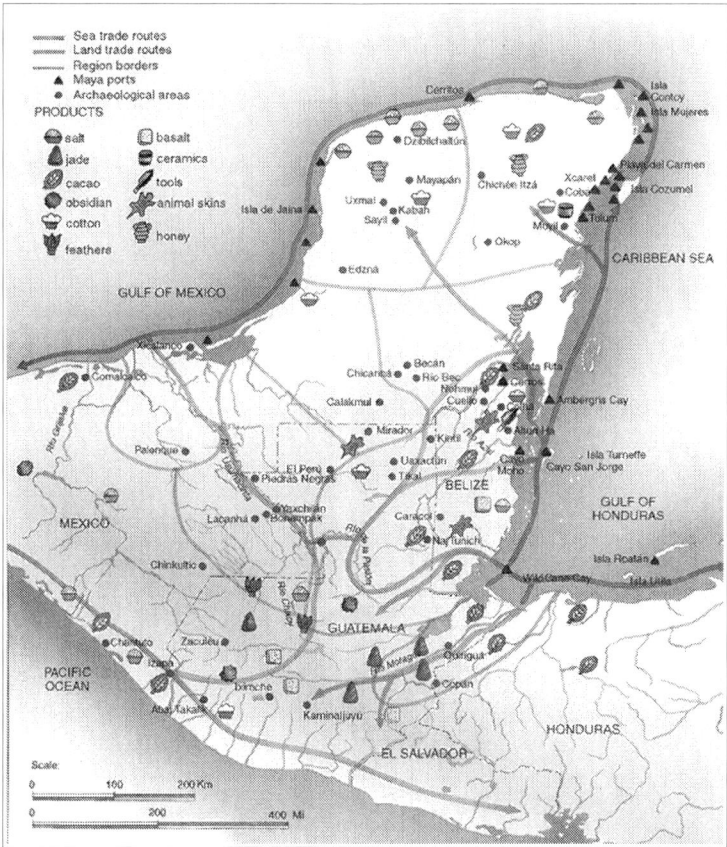

*Regular Maya Trade Routes.*[249]

The late Preclassic Maya culture included the use of mathematics that were incorporated in the recording of time over long periods which allowed the creation and usage of calendars. Their own writing system progressed and spread with their culture.

It is during this time that the production of vertically standing monolithic rocks called stelae (singular stela) and other carved monuments such as alters were now being created. These monuments were initially produced in the highlands and along the Pacific coastal regions, but quickly spread to other regions. Stelae have been found throughout the Maya area in every major preclassic Maya settlement.

Various other permanent carving were also starting to be produced in other parts of the Maya region. A stucco mask tradition had formed in the lowlands of Belize and Peten with masks flanking the stairways of their temples.

During the Late Preclassic period elaborately carved monumental architecture becomes more common. The earliest corbelled vaults (false arches) were being carved within enclosed tombs by important temples.

Ceramic styles also become more uniform cross-regionally and the production of pottery that was painted in three or more colors becomes both widespread and popular. Most of the new painted pottery was placed in the tombs and burials of elite rulers whom were now displaying marked differences in status with their subjects.

Their stories and the significant events in their

lives were now being depicted and dated by their calendars.

There have been surviving late preclassic murals that have provided important information regarding Maya religion and of the rituals they practiced for royal inaugurations that date to around 100 BC.

*Mural from Maya House at Xultun, northern Guatemala.*[83]

All of these carved altars, works of stelae, wall carvings and preserved stucco works have shown us how much the Maya's culture and technology has progressed. The Maya civilization was reaching its zenith of development in the late Preclassic period when a great portion of their civilization suddenly disappeared or perished.

It is well known that the Maya civilization had long disappeared and their culture long had been lost for over 500 years. This was the aftermath of the Spanish conquest of Mesoamerica by Spanish

Conquistadors. But the Spanish reported that there were already Maya cites that had been abandoned long before they had even arrived. The Spaniards had found the ruins of cities that were completely abandoned with no trace of being recently inhabited.

The story of the mysterious lost civilization that seemed to suddenly collapse for unknown reasons has puzzled archaeologists for well over half a millennium. There were actually two 'collapses' of the Maya civilization. The first one was at the end of the Preclassic period and the well known second occurrence at the end of the Classic period with the arrival of the Spanish.

The first collapse was at the end of the late preclassic period with the systematic decline and abandoning of some major city-states such as the ones at Kaminaljuyu and El Mirador sometime around 100 AD.[12] It is unknown why these cities were abandoned and left in ruins. There are a number of theories as to why these cities may have become emptied, but there is little consensus. Some believe that it was possibly war between rival Maya city-states or even perhaps from neighboring civilizations. There could have been a pandemic of disease brought on by famine with over demanding populations that were not able to cope. There is also a probability that a natural disaster, such hurricanes, could have wiped these cities into ruin.

Although a portion of the Maya civilization had collapsed with an unexplained disappearance; the remaining Maya city-states continued to progress into the height of their culture during the Classic period.

# Chapter 8

## The Classic Period (200 AD - 900 AD)

During the Classic period, the ancient Maya culture was flourishing in Mesoamerica. They were at the height of their splendor. So of their architecture changed and they began constructing buildings that paid homage to their rulers and gave reverence to their ancestors. This was the Classic Maya Period, a time between 200 AD and 900 AD when city-states were expressing their power by creating unique architectural centers that in many ways were meant to replicate their cosmology.

Paying homage to important ancestors was critical to their beliefs. One of the most important social acts for a new king was to establish their relationship with the founder of their lineage. Rulers did so by sponsoring the creations of magnificent works of art that shown their link to the ancestors and gods.[81]  These are some of the works that have left clues behind for us to explore and learn the about the Maya's story.

During most of the Classic period, the population of the Maya people continued to grow, especially in and around urban centers of kingdoms and city-states.  The Snake Kingdom of Calakmul had at least a population of 50,000 or more people under their governance during the Classic period.

The Snake Kingdom was a ruled by a powerful dynasty and reached as far as in places that were 150 kilometers away from its capital in Calakmul.  The Snake Kingdom had built many structures.  There are 6,750 ancient structures identified at Calakmul alone. The largest structure built by this dynasty was the great pyramid at the Calakmul site.  The Great Pyramid of Calakmul is also known as 'Structure 2.' It is one of the tallest of all the Maya temple pyramids.

The Great Pyramid at Calakmul.[82]

Most historians mark 300 AD as the beginning of the Maya Classic period because this was when the appearance of stelae began. The earliest stela dates to 292 AD. A stela is a carved vertical stone statue of an important king or ruler.

*Stela of the Great King Waxaklajun Ubaah K'awii (18 Rabbits)in Copan.*[225]

Stelae include not only a likeness of the ruler, but they also have a written record of his accomplishments in the form of glyphs carved on stone.  Stelae became common in the larger Maya cites that thrived during this time.  The Maya began to build multistoried temples, pyramids and palaces during this period of time.  Many of the temples they had built were aligned with the Sun and stars.  With the aid of their accurate calendars they would plan important ceremonies that took place when the temples were aligned with the right celestial objects.

This was a time in Mesoamerica when many forms of art thrived.  Maya artisans were creating finely carved pieces of jade.  They painted large murals and created finely detailed stone carvings in many forms.  They also made finely painted ceramics and pottery that have survived to this day and time.  Their level of complexity and artistic creativity was at an all time high.

During the year 258 AD, the Tutul-Xius, a princely family from Tulha, suddenly left Guatemala and appeared in the Yucatán Peninsula.  It is uncertain as to why they had migrated and if it was related to the portion of the Maya civilization that had mysteriously collapsed in that part of the region.  They may have been seeking refuge from war, the reason is never told in any of the recordings found of the Tutul-Xius family.

The Tutul-Xius had won over the good will of the Mayapan king and pledged themselves as his loyal vassals. The Tutul-Xius family, then founded the cities of Mani and Tihoo, They also founded the great city of Mérida which came with all its splendor. This architecture of this city displays the height and beauty of the Classical period Maya civilization.

Like many Greek city-states, the Maya city-states had their own gods they revered as favoring the inhabitants of the city. Keeping these gods happy, kept the whole Maya World happy.

In the city of Tihoo, 'Baklum-Chaam' was the deity most revered. Backlum Chaam was the god of male sexuality. He was the Maya version of the Greek god Priapu. The Maya had built a great temple as a sanctuary to this god.

Many of the larger cities and capitals had multiple gods to appease, including the greater gods. In the city of Izamal, a great pyramid was built to the Maya Sun God named, "Kinich-Kak-Mo." The Maya called this sacred temple, "Yahan-Kuna," meaning 'most beautiful temple.'

The city of Mérida was considered one of the most advanced Maya cites that contained some of the most beautiful buildings in the whole extent of country. This was how by the Spanish described it when they came upon this city a thousand years later. They were in awe of its beauty and the splendor of the city's elaborate architecture.

The Spaniards described some of the buildings as being thirty feet high and made of finely constructed hammered stone that was laid without cement. On the summits of these elaborately decorated buildings were four apartments. Each apartment was divided into 20 x 10 foot cells that had vaulted ceilings.

The Spanish priests were so pleased with the beauty of this architecture that they established the convent of St. Francis in Mérida and transformed the Maya temple into a Christian chapel for the service of God.[89]

This was how the Maya were building their cities by the Classic period. They were built in such a way that the Spanish were impressed with them over a thousand years after they were built.

Mérida wasn't the only Classic period Maya city rising to greater splendor. Arriving from the west, a prince named Cukulcan established himself at Chichen-Itza and took control of the supreme government of the Snake empire. He established Mayapan as the empire's capital city.

*The Great Pyramid in the Maya city of Chichen Itza.*[108]

By Cukulcan's management, the government was divided into three absolute sovereignties. These sovereignties would upon occasion act together and form one. The seven succeeding sovereigns of Mayapan embellished upon this king's ideas and improved the country, making Mayapan very prosperous.

At this time the city of Uxmal, governed by one of the Tutul-Xius, began to rival the city of Mayapan in extent of territory and in the number of its vassals. The towns of Noxcacab, Kabah, Bocal and Nŏhpat were among its dependencies.

The city of Uxmal was founded in 864 AD, according to Maya dating. It was during this period that great avenues paved with stone started being constructed and laid out. The most remarkable of these extends from the interior of the Maya area to the shores of the sea opposite of Cozumel. There were stone paved roads that led to Izamal which were constructed specifically for the convenience of pilgrims.

This was during a time when a long peace existed between the reigning princes of the several linked principal cities. The peace was eventually brought to an end when an alliance formed against the King of Mayapan.

The rulers of Chichen and Uxmal dared to openly condemn the conduct of the king of Mayapan, whose tyrannical exactions forced him to hire bodyguards to protect himself from his own people. He moved to Kimpech, upon which he bestowed upon himself the entire town and its neighborhood as his residence alone. All the inhabitants were now his servants whose royal favors were to serve him.

His people were especially outraged by the introduction of slavery, which had been previously unknown to them. The alliance managed to unseat him, but a change of rulers at Mayapan failed to settle the troubles within the Snake empire. So a conspiracy formed of independent princes and the new tyrant of Mayapan was deposed of after finally being defeated in a three day battle inside the city of Mayapan. The palace was taken and the king and his family were brutally murdered. The city was then put to flames and was left a vast and desolate heap of ruins.

One of the Tutul-Xius princes of Uxmal was then crowned with the title of supreme monarch of the Maya upon his return from vanquishing the second tyrant king.

This new king governed the country with great wisdom and extended his protection over the foreign mercenaries of the former tyrant. He offered them a place of asylum not far from his city of Uxmal. These areas are now the remains of the towns Pockboc, Sakbache and Lebna. During this time the city of Mayapan was then rebuilt and existed to a lesser extent of its former greatness.

Unfortunately, the city of Mayapan was later again the cause of dissension within the Snake kingdom and in 1464 AD was once again destroyed. After its destruction, a peace settled in the Yucatan for more than twenty years. It was during this period of time that there was great abundance and prosperity. At the end of this time, the country was subjected to a series of disasters. Hurricanes came and reaped incalculable damage upon the cities. The population was hit by plagues that brought great destruction of life. This was the beginning of the rapid depopulation of the peninsula. It wasn't but shortly after these great natural disasters and plagues that the Spaniards arrived. The existence of Mesoamerican power in Yucatan came to an end at this point.[90]

The Maya late Classic period during the years 600 through to 900 AD was the high point of Maya culture. Their art, culture, and religion reached their peaks and influenced cultures around them. They had powerful city-states like Tikal and Calakmul that dominated the regions around them. They were much like the Greek city-states, in that the Maya city-states also warred with each other. Occasionally they were allied and traded with one another. There may have been as many as eighty Maya city-states during this time. The cities were controlled by an elite ruling class and their priests whom claimed to be directly descended from the Sun, Moon, stars, and planets.

The cities were holding more people than they could support. Trade for food as well as luxury items was brisk and steadily fed into the center markets. Much as the dilemma that had fallen upon the Romans in their great cities, there became a need to pacify the masses. Public rituals became the norm and ceremonial games came about. The ceremonial ball game became a major feature of all Maya cities.

It was during the Classic period that the ancient

Maya ballgame called 'pitz' or 'pok-ta-pok' came around. This ballgame was a very important part of Maya political, religious and social life.

*An illustration showing the sacred Maya ball game being played.*[226]

The game was played with a rubber ball ranged in size from being as small as a softball to as big as a soccer ball. The game was played with two teams that would attempt to score by bouncing the rubber ball through stone hoops attached to the sides of the ball court. The players could only use their bodies and had to bounce the ball without using their hands

The ball court itself was a focal point of Maya cities and symbolized the city's wealth and power based upon its size and grandeur. The prestige of a city's ball court became as important to the Maya as were their pyramids and temples. They built grand ball courts to hold the games in great public ritual with all the splendor the city had to offer.

*Illustration of the Ball Court at Copán, Honduras.*[234]

The Mesoamerican ball game is estimated to have been played by many pre-Columbian civilizations in Mesoamerica for over 3,600 years. The ball game was considered a sport, but it was mainly a ritual that was conducted to please the gods. The Maya ball game pok-ta-pok was also played by the Aztec in Mexico, where it was called 'tlachtli.'

Tlachtli was the ball game witnessed being played by Spanish conquistadors whom would later describe in their journals. The ball game was very popular with the people in Mesoamerica. The ball game called batey was played by the islanders of the Greater Antilles. The game played by rubber balls is known to have reached as far south as modern day Paraguay and as far north as to the current state of Arizona.

With the game being played in Mesoamerica for over 3,600 years, it is inevitable that local variations would appear as the game spread to different cultures. The ball game seen by the conquistadors in the 16th century would certainly have differed in several ways from the games that were played much earlier when the game started.

*The ball in front of the goal during a Maya game of pok-ta-pok.*[275]

Pre-Columbian ball courts have been found throughout Mesoamerica. These ball courts varied considerably in size depending on the size of the city that built them. Regardless of size, they all were built with long narrow alleys that had inward sloped side-walls where the balls could bounce. They also all had stone rings hanging high on the walls for the balls to be bounced through.

The Great Ball Court located in the city of Chichén Itzá is the largest one ever found in all of Mesoamerica. This ball court had an I-shaped playing ground that was 150 meters long with a small temple located at each end.

The ball court, called poctapoc, was very elaborated decorated. There are relief carvings on the lower walls of the ball court depicting ball game activities and ritual sacrifice. At each end of the ball court were small decorated temples and the Temple of the Bearded Man was in front of the court. Another great mystery of the Maya was the temples and carving of 'the bearded man,' as Mesoamericans did not have facial hair.

*Sculpture in the Temple of the Warriors at Chichén Itzá.* [74]

The acoustics of this structure allow a person standing at one end of the court to be speaking in a natural voice to be heard by another person standing about 150 yards away at the other end of the ball court.

It is not specifically known how the Maya ball game was played, but according to the most widespread version of it, the goal of the game was to pass the ball through one of the rings without touching it. The rules were that the players needed to strike the ball with their hips.

At the Great Ball Court located in Chichén Itzá, they used a solid rubber ball that was about 20 inches in diameter and weighed about 9 lbs or more. It was extremely difficult to get the ball through a ring. In fact, when a player managed to get the ball through the hoop, the game ended with the scored point. The game or possibly the round ended when the ball touched the ground.

The ball game was often played for recreational sport, but major formal ball games were held as ritual events that often featured human sacrifice. There was a high ritual importance behind the Maya ball game of pok-ta-pok. It was a formal religious ceremony that involved the participation of not only religious leaders, but nobility and other important officials. They sang sacred songs and preformed ceremonial dances at these events.

The game was played by two opposing teams, one team was shadow and the other was light. It is believed that the game's winners were given a great feast and hailed as heroes. The losers did not have it as well, as the penalty for losing a game was death. The captain of the losing team was sacrificed It is believed that the sacrificed captain would have a place of honor within the neighboring structure in the Temple of Warriors.

The Maya believed that human sacrifice was necessary for obtaining continued success in agriculture, trade and general health. If the gods did not get human blood to quench their thirst, then they punished the population and in some cases, would destroy the World.[274]

The Maya civilization began to wane towards the end of the Classic period. Nobody knows exactly why, but it has been a continuing mystery to archaeologists for hundreds of years. Around the year 800 AD, the once thriving Maya civilization of Mesoamerica began to rapidly collapse. There were a series of catastrophic volcanic eruptions that had devastated the countryside. This was followed by two extreme droughts that lasted for long periods of time. This goes without mentioning the unending wars that occurred between city-states.

There is evidence of erosion in soils going up slopes. This tells us that farmers had to spread to steeper ground with less suitable soils. Maya agricultural demands did cause substantial erosion of their usable soil. This loss could eventually have undercut their ability to grow enough food to meet their population's demand.[240]

The cities in the highlands were the first to be abandoned. This was an area where for over 16 centuries, the Itza Maya farmers were able to produce an abundance of food on mountainside terraces. It was from their ability to produce an abundance of agricultural surpluses that the great cities in the Maya Lowlands and in the Yucatan Peninsula were able to grow so large and prosperous.

With the combination of natural disasters, such as volcanic eruptions and hurricanes, the addition of wars and then drought eradicated the abundance of food. The densely populated Maya lowlands were now stricken with famine. This caused more wars and greater starvation so that within the period of a century, most of the cities became abandoned.

Some of the cities in the far north were taken over by the Itza Maya and these city-states continued to thrive for two more centuries. The city of Tikal became an urban center of great importance for the late classic Maya. Some of the landscaping and engineering feats in this city include the largest ancient dam that was ever built by the Maya.

*Veneer stones belonging to an ancient Maya dam.*[243]

The dam was constructed using a combination of cut stone, rubble and earth. The dam stretched in length for more than 260 feet and held about 20 million gallons of water in a human-made reservoir with 33 foot high walls.

There were periods of excessive rainfall that coincided with a rise in population from 300 to 660 AD. The Maya had to learn to conserve and use their natural resources wisely in order to support a very populous and highly complex society despite the many environmental challenges, which included periodic droughts.[241]

Large-scale alterations in the landscape plus the

high demands placed on resources from an ecosystem that caused an extreme amount of stress on environmental conditions. This caused the ever growing harsher conditions to become amplified by increasing amount of climatic aridity developing.

These events made economic and environmental conditions quickly change which caused an increasing amount of social conflict in the region. A climate reversal occurred and a drying trend began to take place at around 660 AD. These adverse conditions triggered political competition and increased warfare. By 1000 AD, the overall sociopolitical instability finally pushed to the Maya elite to diminish control of the cities and migrate elsewhere in the peninsular region. They could not meet the high costs of maintaining the cities with an environment that could no longer sustain the human demand.

Even the flow of commerce had shifted from crossing the peninsula over land and through the wastelands to moving by sea to go around and avoid it. After the central Maya lowlands were finally abandoned, the environment began to largely recover. However, the Maya population never fully recovered after this period.[242]

This was followed by another extended drought that happened between 1020 to 1100 AD.

This drought likely caused huge crop failures that resulted in a famine that caused many deaths. More mass migration out of the areas was ultimately the collapse of the Maya population before the arrival of the Spanish.[244]

Hurricanes have played a key role in much of the devastation that has taken place throughout history of Belize and the Yucatan peninsula. The 'Maya Area' has long been hit with large, devastating hurricanes and tropical storms.

In modern history, a hurricane in 1931 destroyed over two-thirds of the buildings in Belize City and more than 1,000 people had died in that storm. In 1955, 'Hurricane Janet' leveled the northern town of Corozal, Belize. It was only six years later when they were still recovering and rebuilding when "Hurricane Hattie" struck the central coastal area. This hurricane struck the countryside with 300-kph winds and storm tides that were over four meters high.

The devastation of Belize City for the second time in thirty years prompted the relocation of the Belizean capital to be moved 50 miles inland to the planned city of Belmopan. Relocating cities and resettling survivors had occurred several times with the ancient Maya as a result of some of the violent hurricanes they'd experienced.

In 1978, 'Hurricane Greta' hit along the southern coast and then 'Hurricane Iris' made landfall on October 9, 2001. This was a category 4 storm with 145 mph winds that had demolished most of the homes in a village and destroyed the banana crop. It was these kinds of storms that hit the ancient Maya and destroyed their homes and crops. This explains why some regions in the Maya area were periodically abandoned.

In 2007, the category 5 hurricane 'Dean' made landfall north of the Belize/Mexico border and caused extensive damage in northern Belize. Then just three years later, a category 2 level hurricane made landfall approximately 20 miles south-southeast of Belize City on October 25, 2010. That hurricane caused millions of dollars of damage to many crops and buildings.

These modern examples of hurricanes wiping out entire regions would have had an even heavier affect on the Maya, whom if there were any survivors, would have had to abandon the area because all their crops, food stores, possessions, buildings, and any form of livelihood they had would have been completely wiped out.

Areas that would have been wiped out and cleared by hurricane storms, would have been quickly reclaimed by the jungle. This explains why there were reports made by exploring Spaniards of finding regularly overgrown and abandoned Maya cities. These reports were from the first Europeans entering the area. They explain the hardships that they'd endured from storms, including many shipwrecks that resulted from these storms. The often very extreme weather explains the lack of population densities in the Maya area and why there wasn't any real long term success of anything that was man-made in the region.

# Chapter 9

## The Post-Classic Period

## (900 AD - 1697 AD)

The Post-Classic Period is the time between the year 900 AD and the conquest of Mesoamerica by the Spaniards between 1521 and 1697 AD. The Post-Classic era was a period in Maya history where military activity became of great importance in order to meet the drastically changing political climate. It was during this time that the political elites were once associated with the priestly class had been relieved of power by groups of warriors.

During the Post-Classic period, at least a half century before the arrival of the Spaniards, the Maya warrior class had yielded its positions of privilege to a very powerful group that were unconnected to the nobility called the "Pochtecas." The Pochtecas were merchants whom had obtained great political power through their economic power. Similar of the modern age, where entities of vast acquired wealth and influence are able to place themselves into positions of power and control. This is what the Pochtecas had done.

These merchants of the Post-Classic period had possessed substantial amounts of wealth and commodities. It was during times of great need and desperation that these wealthy merchants were easily able to seat themselves as rulers. When a current ruling noble house has fallen or lost its influence over the local population, the Pochtecas were swift to move in.

The early part of the Post-Classic period was a period of time characterized by Toltec influence whom had their capital in Tula featuring the Pyramid of Quetzalcoatl, the great shrine to the feathered serpent god. The Toltecs were just north of the Maya and had quickly grown in power and influence. They dominated and influenced much of Mesoamerica until the late 12th century when they fell from power.

The late Post-Classic period begins during the late 12th century, after the Toltec were gone and the

Chichimec people began to arrive. These people were linguistically related to the Toltecs and to the Mexica people. They'd begun moving into Mesoamerica and encroaching upon the Maya, whom themselves were already being pushed north because of the changed environment.

These migratory movements by northern people were the result of not just the environment, but of the many social changes that took place during the final period of Mesoamerican civilization. These people came from the northern regions of Mesoamerica were driven by climate changes that threatened their own survival. These migrations from the north caused displacement of many people whom were already permanently settled in the area. Cultures that had been firmly rooted in parts of Mesoamerica for centuries. These newcomers from the north were also bringing their religion and culture with them. These changes had profound influences on the Maya and other Mesoamericans.

There were many cultural changes that took place during the post-classic period. One of them was the introduction and spread of knowledge about metallurgy. Metallurgy was introduced to the Maya sometime at around 800 AD. This knowledge was actually imported from South American cultures whom had already been experimenting with metals.

The Maya did not achieve great expertise with the use of metals. Metal had been occasionally used to make a few trinket items, but wasn't experimented with in general. Most Mesoamericans limited their use of metals to creating jewelry and some tools. New alloys and techniques had been developed in a few centuries later, but metal had little use or value to them.

The most advanced techniques of Mesoamerican metallurgy were developed by the Mixtecos, whom had been influenced by northern cultures. They produced many exquisite handcrafted items from metal, especially that of fine jewelry. Gem setting was one of the Mesoamerican popular uses of metal.

Metal took on a slow role in development in Mesoamerica. It wasn't until later when they began using metals with construction, such as using nails to secure parts of buildings. There were great improvements in mortar and its usage, which allowed for improved construction methods. The Maya began using support columns in their buildings and stone roofs became commonplace in the progressive Maya areas in the post classic period.

Their system of agricultural irrigation became more and more complex to meet their population's demand. In the valley of Mexico, 'chinampas' were used to grow food.

*Depiction of Chinampas.*[286]

Chinampas were made by using creating small rectangular areas on shallow lake beds and putting fertile arable soil on top to grow crops. They used small rafts to pole their way between them. This method was used extensively in the valley of Mexico by the Mexica people to grow a majority of their food. The Mexica had built over 200,000 chinampas around their city to meet their agricultural needs.

The political system throughout Mesoamerica had undergone major changes during the early Post-Classic period. Many warlike political elites were now legitimizing their positions by means of a strict adherence to a complex set of religious beliefs they had learned from the Toltec culture.[155] According to this system, the ruling classes proclaimed themselves to being the direct descendants of the god Quetzalcoatl. They had an entire priest class back their claims of lineage to highly revered. The Plumed Serpent, Quetzalcoatl was one of the creative forces of the universe and also a cultural hero in Mesoamerican mythology and culture. Being able to claim lineage to this god gave the ruler unquestionable right to reign.

These new rulers also declared themselves to be the heirs of a mythical city of the gods called, "Zuyuá" in Mayan. Another feature of the newly adopted religious system was that it allowed the formation of alliances with other city-states that were controlled by groups that had the same ideology.

This was the case with the League of Mayapán in Yucatán. These northern Maya and neighboring cultures had united under religion. This was same with the Mixtec confederation of Lord Eight Deer, based north of the Maya in the mountains of Oaxaca. At this point in the Post-Classic period, many Mesoamerican societies can be characterized by their military nature and multi-ethnic populations.

The fall of Tula and the militaristic Toltec checked the power in the new religious system. The alliances broke down with the dissolution of the League of Mayapán. The Mixtec state unification fell apart as well the abandonment of religious leadership coming from Tula.

Mesoamerica was now receiving new immigrants from northern regions. These groups of people from the north were related to the ancient Toltecs, but had completely different ideologies than the existing residents. The final arrivals to the Mesoamerican region before the coming of the Spanish were the Mexica. They'd established themselves on a small island on Lake Texcoco under the dominion of the Texpanecs of Azcapotzalco.

The Mexica arrived and settled, then later conquered a large part of Mesoamerica They then created a unified and centralized state. A centralized empire whose only rivals were the Tarascan state of Michoacán. Neither one of these people could defeat each other in warfare. Both had tried to defeat the other several times. The military stalemate led the way to creating a loose non-aggression pact between the two people.

When the Spaniards arrived in Mesoamerica, many of the people that were controlled by the Mexica, no longer wished to remain under their rule. They seen the arrival of the conquering Spaniards as an opportunity to free themselves and agreed to support the Europeans in their conquest against the Mexica. They thought that in return for helping the Spanish that they'd gain their freedom. They had no idea that they were assisting in the entire subjugation of all the Mesoamerican world by the European newcomers.

The Post-Classic Era saw the collapse of many of the great Mesoamerican nations and Maya city-states that had dominated the region during the Classic Era. Not all of them had perished during the post classic period before the arrival of the Spanish. The Maya of the Yucatán continued to exist as a distinct culture and in many cases their great cities at Chichen Itza and Uxmal thrived. However, this was a period of increased social chaos and warfare.

The Post-Classic was a time of technological advancement in architecture, engineering and weaponry, but it was also a period of cultural decline. However, it was during the Post-Classic period that Mesoamerica experienced rapid movements and growths in population, this was especially true in Central Mexico after 1200 AD. It was also a time of experimentation in governance.

For example, in Yucatán, 'dual rulership' apparently replaced the more theocratic governments of Classic times. Post classic era seen oligarchic councils controlled by the few elite now controlled much of Central Mexico. The wealthy 'pochteca' merchants backed by military orders had become more powerful than they were during the

Classic period. This afforded some Mesoamericans a degree of social mobility that would have otherwise never presented it's self.

By the 1400's, there was a renewal of Maya populations spreading in Southern Yucatán and Guatemala. There was a renaissance of fine arts and science as the culture flourished. Just north of the regrowing Maya was the Aztec Empire that had risen to power in the early 15th century.

The Aztec were on a fast path to exerting their dominance over the entire Mexico valley region until Mesoamerica had been discovered by Spanish explorers. The Post Preclassic period ended shortly after the discovery and the arrival of Spanish conquistadors. The start of the 16$^{th}$ century would have a profound impact on the entirety of Mesoamerica to the point of extinction of many native cultures.

In 1492, Christopher Columbus sailed across the ocean and discovered the Bahamas. He named and claimed these islands 'San Salvador,' on behalf of the Kingdom of Spain (Castile and Leon). He encountered an indigenous people on the islands, whom were peaceful and friendly. He spoke of them in his journal.

On October 12, 1492, Christopher Columbus wrote:

*"Many of the men I have seen have scars on their bodies, and when I made signs to them to find out how this happened, they indicated that people from other nearby islands come to San Salvador to capture them; they defend themselves the best they can. I believe that people from the mainland come here to take them as slaves. They ought to make good and skilled servants, for they repeat very quickly whatever we say to them. I think they can very easily be made Christians, for they seem to have no religion. If it pleases our Lord, I will take six of them to Your Highnesses when I depart, in order that they may learn our language."*[85]

Columbus also remarked that their lack of modern weaponry and tactical vulnerability in writing:

*"I could conquer the whole of them with 50 men, and govern them as I pleased."*[86]

Columbus also explored the northeast coast of Cuba, where he landed and also claimed for Spain on October 28, 1492. It was during Columbus' second voyage in 1494, that he passed along the southern coast of the Cuban island and landed at various inlets including what was later to become Guantanamo Bay.

After receiving news of the discoveries upon Columbus' return, King Ferdinand and Queen Isabella of Spain urged Pope Alexander VI to confirm their right of possession to all of the newly discovered lands in the Americas. The Pope was persuaded and in the Papal Bull of 1493, known as the Doctrine of Discovery, Pope Alexander VI commanded Spain to conquer, colonize and convert the pagans in the New World to Catholicism.[87][88]

Private adventurers and investors scrambled to enter into contracts with the Spanish Crown in order to conquer the newly discovered lands in return for tax revenues and the power to rule.[60] The Spanish had quickly colonized the Caribbean and established their center of operations on the island of Cuba within the first decades after the initial discovery of the New World.

The Spanish heard rumors of a rich empire to the west belonging to the Aztec on the mainland of the New World. Hernán Cortés then set sail the coast of Mexico with eleven ships in 1519 to seek out this rich empire of the Aztec. By August 1521, the Aztec empire had fallen and their capital of Tenochtitlan was conquered by the Spanish. Then within a three year period after the fall of the Aztec capital, the Spanish had conquered a large part of Mexico.

This newly conquered Mesoamerican territory became New Spain, known as the Viceroyalty of New Spain, from 1521 until the end of Spanish control in 1821. New Spain was governed by a viceroy whom only answered to the King of Spain through of the Spanish Empire's Royal and Supreme Council of the Indies.

Further desiring to expand conquered territory, Cortés dispatched Pedro de Alvarado with an army to conquer the Mesoamerican kingdoms in the Guatemalan Sierra Madre and neighboring Pacific plain. This was the military phase of the establishment of the Spanish colony of Guatemala which lasted from 1524 to 1541.[61]

When the colony was formed, the Captaincy General of Guatemala established its capital at Santiago de los Caballeros de Guatemala. This colony governed a wide territory that included the modern day Mexican state of Chiapas, and the modern nations of El Salvador, Honduras and Costa Rica.[62]

The Spanish had imposed strict colonial rule over the Yucatán region from 1527 to 1546 . They had later gained control over Verapaz and ruled it from the 16th to 17th centuries. They left the area between Petén and most of Belize independent long after the surrounding people had been subjugated.[63]

Bernal Díaz del Castillo was the chronicler who gave the most detail about the voyage of Hernández de Córdoba. Bernal dates March 4, 1517 as the first encounter with the indigenous people of the Yucatán

Saying the Spaniards asked the natives for the name of the land they'd just arrived upon and the natives replied in their language saying, "Tectetán," which means, "I don't understand you." The Spaniards did not understand what the natives were saying, so took their word Tectetán and mispronounced it, 'Yucatán' as being the name of the land.[92]

The same happened with a cape made by the land there. When inquiring about the structures the Spaniards spotted, the natives responded with, "Catoche," meaning "our houses." The Spanish mistook this for the name of the settlement and the cape where they had arrived.

# Chapter 10

## The Spanish Conquest of the Maya

First contact between the Spanish and the Maya occurred in the year 1511. This was 19 years after Columbus discovered the Bahamas in 1492. The first contact between the Spanish and the Maya occurred after a shipwreck had brought the survivors to Maya shores. The written account of the shipwreck and of the events that followed are written in Bernal Díaz's, "Verdadera Historia de la Conquista de Nueva España" (in english: True History of the Conquest of New Spain).[50]

Many of the details written by Díaz differ than the accounts given from other 16th century chroniclers, such as Cervantes, Gómara, and Martyr. All of whom differ in their accounts of the number aboard the ship, how many survivors had reached the shore, and the ultimate fate of said survivors. They do, however, all agree that ultimately at least two of them had survived the shipwreck and the events that followed.

The first known Spanish landing on the Yucatán Peninsula and first contact with the Maya was the result of a catastrophe happening at sea. A small ship from Darién Panama sailing to Santo Domingo on Hispaniola had run aground on some shoals in the Caribbean Sea just south of the island of Jamaica in 1511.[51] There were fifteen men and two women aboard this damaged ship. They abandoned ship and attempted to set off in the ship's boat to try to reach Hispaniola or one of the other Spanish colonies.

Their attempts to reach any Spanish colonies failed when prevailing currents carried them westwards. The ship survivors drifted helplessly with the current for two weeks. Eventually the current carried them to land, where they arrived somewhere on the eastern shoreline of the Yucatán Peninsula. The exact location of their landing is not known, but it could have possibly been somewhere along the coast of present-day Belize.[52]

The shipwreck survivors made it to land and were swiftly captured by some local Maya and were then divided up as slaves among several of the chieftains. A number of the surviving Spanish shipwreck crew were also sacrificed according to customary Maya offertory practices.[53]

Over the following years their numbers began to dwindle when some died from disease or because of exhaustion from being overworked. Eventually there were only two men left. The two remaining survivors were Gerónimo de Aguilar and Gonzalo Guerrero. Aguilar had managed to escape from his captor and found refuge with another Maya ruler. Gonzalo Guerrero managed to win over some prestige among the Maya for his bravery. Guerrero achieved the standing of a ranking Maya warrior and granted the status of a noble.

These two men would later play two very different roles in future conflicts between the Spanish and the Maya people. Gerónimo de Aguilar would become Hernán Cortés' Mayan translator and an adviser in assisting Spain conquer the Maya states. Gonzalo Guerrero would remain with the Maya people, serving as a tactician and as a warrior fighting with them against the Spanish.

The next contact between the Spaniards and the Maya happened in the year 1517, when the Spanish conquistador Francisco Hernández de Córdoba sailed to the Yucatán from Cuba in search of slaves to replace the native Cuban slaves that were dying off in great numbers. The Spaniards were surprised to see stone cities along the coast of Yucatán. Córdoba and his men landed at several locations. Some of the Maya greeted the Spaniards with friendship and offered to trade goods with them. The Spaniards were lucky to acquire a few pieces of gold ornaments by trading.

However, the Spaniards weren't always friendly greeted by the Maya, such as the incident at Cape Cotoche when the explorers landed at the coast to gather fresh water inland. Córboda and his men were ambushed with about 80 Spaniards being wounded by a volley of stones, arrows, and darts. The Spanish quickly learned that even though the Maya arrows weren't attaining any distinct force behind them, they still tended to shatter on impact which lead to a slow and painful death.

Ultimately, the Spaniards had failed in their attempts to gather water and repair their water casks. Córdoba was forced to redistribute the remaining of his men on other ships and abandon his smallest ship, a brigantine which had paid for on credit.[54]

The expedition returned to Cuba to report on the discovery of this new land and of the incident at the Cape. Diego Velázquez, whom was governor of

Cuba, ordered four ships out on an expedition of 240 men to this land. They were supplied with crossbows, muskets, salt pork, and cassava bread . The expedition was led by his nephew, Juan de Grijalva.[55] The Grijalva expedition experienced similar relations with the native Maya, some were friendly and some being hostile. Grijalva was genuinely anxious to fulfill Velázquez' order to explore the new lands rather than conquer.

Except for occasionally firing a few cannon shots out of spite, Grijalva repeatedly denied himself and his men the gratification of vengeance from periodic attacks they received from some Maya as they sailed along the coast of the Yucatán for months. Occasionally a friendly group would exchange beads and Spanish wine for food and other necessities the expedition required. Grijalva was disappointed at the fact that they'd gathered very little gold on their trip; but when they came back to Cuba he shared a tale of hearing about a rich empire that was further to the west inland.

This story prompted Hernán Cortés to lead an expedition into the Yucatán in 1519. Cortés had spent some time at the island of Cozumel off the coast of the Yucatán where he tried to convert the locals to Christianity, but had limited and mixed results. This was when he'd heard the rumors of other 'bearded white men' that were living in the area. Cortés sent messengers to these 'bearded white men' whom turned out to be Gerónimo de Aguilar and Gonzalo Guerrero, the last two survivors of the 1511 shipwreck. Upon receiving Cortés message, Aguilar petitioned his Maya chieftain to be allowed to leave and join his former countrymen. The Chieftain agreed to release him and Aguilar made his way to where Cortés and his men's ships were located.

Gerónimo de Aguilar claimed that he tried to convince Guerrero to leave with him, but failed. Guerrero was now already well-assimilated into the Maya culture and was looked upon as a figure of rank by the local Maya. Aguilar claimed that Guerrero had a Maya wife and three children at the Maya settlement of Chetumal where he was now living.[56]

Aguilar would prove himself to be a valuable asset as a translator for Cortés expedition into the Yucatán. He had lived with the Maya for so long that he was now quite fluent in speaking "Yucatec Mayan," along with a few other local indigenous languages.[57]

Gonzalo Guerrero's fate was never known. It is assumed that for some years that he fought alongside the Maya warriors against the Spanish Conquistadors. He provided the Maya with military counsel on tactics to fight and resist the Spanish invasion. Although unconfirmed, Guerrero is believed to have later been killed in a battle.

However, Hernán Cortés and some 500 Conquistadors were currently engaged in the richer lands of Mexico. The quest for gold kept the attention of the Spaniards in the Mexico region for a few years. By 1511, the Spanish Conquistadors led by Cortés had defeated the mighty Aztec Empire with the use of modern weapons and the assistance of thousands of Mesoamerican allies.

It was the Spanish Conquistador Pedro de Alvarado whom was granted the privilege of conquering the Maya after he and his brothers had proven themselves in the ranks of Cortes' army. In the year 1523, he set out with approximately four hundred Spanish Conquistadors and about ten-thousand Mesoamerican allies to conquer the Maya.

By the year 1524, Pedro de Alvarado's band of Spanish Conquistadors and his native allies moved into the Maya area which is now present-day Guatemala. The Maya civilization had already deteriorated some centuries before the arrival of the Spanish. Only a number of small kingdoms remained of the once populous Maya city-states.

The strongest of the remaining Maya kingdoms was the kingdom of the K'iche. These people were located in the area that is now central Guatemala. The K'iche people had rallied around a leader named Tecún Umán to defend their lands and met Alvarado's Conquistadors and indigenous allies in battle. Unfortunately, the K'iche lost the battle and were permanently defeated, ending any significant native resistance in the area.

Another Spanish conquistador, Francisco de Montejo had also joined Hernán Cortés in the conquest of Mexico. In 1526, Montejo had successfully petitioned the King of Spain for the right to conquer the Maya of Yucatán. He arrived in eastern Yucatán in 1527 and was at first greeted peaceably by the local Maya. Of the first few settlements that the Spanish encountered, most local chiefs agreed to the Conquistador's demands that they swear oaths of loyalty to the King of Spain. The chieftains agreed because they'd heard news of the Spanish conquest of the Aztecs.

However, as the Spanish advanced further into Maya territory, they found entire cities that were already deserted when they reached them. As the Spanish progressed deeper into the Maya area, they started getting harassed. When they traveled inland even further, they began being openly attacked.

Montejo had his men set up a small fort on the Yucatán coast at 'Xaman Ha' in 1528, but they were unsuccessful in subduing the country and maintain their position. Montejo moved his conquistadors on to Mexico and subdued Tabasco in 1530.

Montejo returned to the Yucatán peninsula in 1531 with a force of conquistadors that were allied with the Maya port city of Campeche.[58] While he set up a fortress in Campeche to base his campaign, he sent his son, Francisco Montejo the Younger (el Mozo), inland with an army to conquer the Maya. As the Conquistador army made their way inland, the leaders of some Maya states pledged that they'd be Spanish allies. Montejo the Younger continued on to Chichen Itza, which he conquered and then declared as the royal capital of the Spanish Yucatán. Only a few months later the locals started to rise up against the Spaniards. The conquistadors were now being constantly attacked, forcing them to eventually flee to Honduras.

It was rumored that Gonzalo Guerrero, the shipwrecked Spaniard that had assimilated with the Maya, was among the Maya warriors helping direct their resistance against the Spanish. Meanwhile, at the fort in Campeche, the elder Montejo was also being frequently besieged and the morale of his men were plummeting. Many of the conquistadors led by the elder Montejo were tired of a long fight with nothing to show for it. They stated that they desired to find easier and more profitable conquests elsewhere.

Meanwhile, the younger Montejo continued to fight the Maya that were becoming more hostile as their numbers grew. They eventually they laid siege to the Spanish barricaded in the city. The Maya were able to cut off the Spanish supply line to the coast and forced them to send for help as they barricaded themselves in the ruins of the ancient city of Chichén Itzá.

Months passed, but no reinforcements came to the aid of the trapped Spaniards. Montejo the Younger attempted an all out assault against the Maya to break their siege and lost 150 of his few remaining forces. He was forced to abandon the city of Chichén Itzá under cover of darkness in 1534.

By the year 1535, Montejo was forced to withdraw his forces to Veracruz and leave the Yucatán once again completely in the control of the Maya. At this point, Francisco de Montejo's men were exhausted, demoralized, and having found no loot after all their efforts, his conquistadors deserted him.

In the year 1540, Montejo, whom has now aged into his late 60's, passed over his rights to conquer the Yucatán by the King of Spain over to his son, Francisco Montejo the Younger. His son immediately renewed the conquest of the Maya and invaded the Yucatán with a renewed large force. By the year 1542, Montejo the Younger had effectively subdued the Western portion of the Yucatán peninsula and then placed his capital in the Maya city of T'ho, which he renamed to Mérida.

The conquered Maya lord of the Tutul Xiu Maya converted to Christianity and swore an oath of loyalty to the King of Spain. The Tutul Xiues had dominated most of the western Yucatán. They became valuable allies to the Spanish, especially against their enemy the Cocom Maya. The Spaniards were in great need of assistance with conquering the rest of the peninsula, as was proven by previous attempts.

The conquest against the Maya in the eastern portion of the Yucatán peninsula came to an end in 1546. With the assistance of the Tutul Xiu, the Spanish defeated a final combined army of mixed forces from the last remaining Maya states in the eastern Yucatán peninsula.

There were a number of Maya states that had pledged loyalty to Spain at first, but they'd later revolt after feeling the heavy hand of Spanish rule. The Maya continued to revolt against their oppressive conquerors for years. There were periodic revolts occurred throughout the Spanish Colonial Era that followed, but they were violently put down by Spanish troops.

The Spanish had unknowingly released a vicious ally ahead of them in their conquest of the New World: disease. The indigenous inhabitants of the New World had no immunity to European diseases such as: smallpox, bubonic plague, chicken pox, mumps and more. These diseases quickly spread through Mesoamerican communities and more than decimated the population.

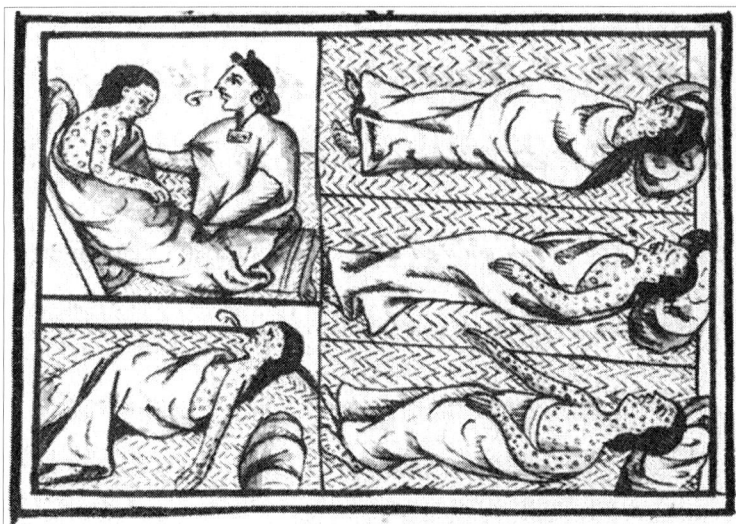

*Drawing of conquest-era Mesoamericans suffering from smallpox.*[72]

It is estimated that more than a third of the Maya population perished from European carried disease between the years 1521 to 1523. But besides the spread of disease, the Spaniards also had other advantages: horses, guns, war dogs, metal armor,

142

steel swords and crossbows. All of these were devastating unknown things to Mesoamericans, of which they were not prepared to defend against.

The arrival of the Spanish brought Mesoamericans the combination of disease, war, slavery and forced relocation that nearly wiped them completely out. Their cultures never recovered. It's estimated that about 88% of the Maya inhabitants died during the first decade of Spanish colonial rule due to a combination of disease and war. Although disease was responsible for the majority of deaths, ruthless warfare between rival Maya groups and Spanish expeditions is what pushed the population over the edge.[64]

The Spanish conquest of the Petén Itza Kingdom was the last stage to conquering Guatemala. The Petén Basin is a wide lowland plain that's covered with a dense tropical rain forest that is now part of modern Guatemala. Cortés had visited this region before during his march to Honduras in 1525. The chieftains of the local Itza Maya that he encountered had all pledged their loyalty to Spain to prevent Cortés from attacking them, but was thereafter neglected as soon as the Spanish left their area.

There had been a few small attempts over the years by the Spanish to convert and conquer the Itza Maya, but all failed. For example, in 1622 the

Spanish Governor of the Yucatán sent a force of twenty Spaniards and 140 converted Christian Maya allies to march on the Itza capital city of Tayasal, but Itza warriors quickly killed them. A similar force was sent to the Petén Basin in 1624 whom were ambushed by Itza warriors and met the same fate as the previous groups.

Due to other areas needing suppressed by other Maya uprisings, the Governor of Yucatán decided his best use of troops and resources would be better spent elsewhere. The Itza Maya continued their independence harassed for the most part through the 17th century. The Itza Maya of the Petén Basin were the last of the significant unconquered Maya kingdoms.[59] The Itza Maya still had significant population that existed in the Petén Basin with most of them living around the central lakes and along the rivers.

The Maya in the Petén were not politically unified as a whole single kingdom. Instead, they were divided into a number of different complex alliances and old rival enmities that were intermixed with other Maya groups in the area.

The most significant groups that were around the Petén central lakes were the Itza, the Yalain and the Kowoj. The other groups whose territories were also in the Petén Basin were the Kejache, Acala,

Lacandon, Xocmo, Chinamita, Icaiche and the Manche Ch'ol.

It was late in the 17th century, when the last Itza Maya ruler began to be more open minded towards the Spaniards. He would receive and protect Spanish emissaries at the capital city of Tayasal. In the year 1695, three Franciscans friars headed to Tayasal and they were well received when they arrived.

A number of the Itza Maya had even consented to being baptized as Christians. However, the Itza King refused to convert to Christianity and pledge his loyalty to Spain. This provoked the Spanish governor of Yucatán to react by sending a force of sixty Spanish soldiers accompanied by Maya allies to the Petén Basin the following year. However, as before, the Spaniards were swiftly beaten back by fierce Itza attacks.

This was when the Spanish governor in the city of Mérida decided that a major force needed to be sent. The following year in 1697 the Spanish Basque conquistador Martín de Ursúa y Arizmendi led a force of 235 Spanish conquistadors and tens of thousands of Xiu Maya marched into the Petén Basin. This time they brought along artillery and a large supply train of mules and men to cut a path through the jungle.

The conquistadors set up a fort on the shore of Lake Petén Itza across from the Itza city of Tayasal and from there they reconstructed a small ship on the lake that they had brought with them that had been disassembled in pieces. Then on March 13, 1697, with everything ready and artillery supporting this large force, they defeated the Itza Maya and seized their capital of Tayasal. The Maya conquest had finally ended with the capture of Tayasal, the island capital of the Itza kingdom.

The Spanish didn't stop at conquering the city, they smashed all the idols of false gods and burned all the Itza Maya's books that 'contained lies of the devil.' The conquistadors reported that there were so many idols within the city that it took them nearly all day to smash them all.

Bishop Landa, whom was with the Conquistadors, described the Maya's books as being large and made with a highly decorated leaf that was doubled in folds which were enclosed between two boards. The Maya wrote on both sides in the columns that were corresponding to the book folds. The paper they used to make their books was made from the roots of a tree, which they put a white varnish on to give a nice surface to write upon.

*The Dresden Codex, 1 of 4 Maya books that survived the Spanish Conquest.*

This art of writing and bookmaking was only known by certain men of high rank. Because of their knowledge in writing and bookmaking, they were held in much esteem by the people.

These writers did not practice their art in public, but the Maya people understood their writings and the meanings behind the characters that they used. The writers taught them and made them understand their meanings. In these books, these writers wrote about their antiquities, myths and of their sciences.

The Spaniards found a great number of these books among the Maya, they were a common item, However, the Spanish believed that these books contained nothing but heretic superstitions and falsities from the devil, so to they burned them all.[91]

*The Pyramid of Kukulcan from the Temple of the Warriors at Chichen-Itza.*[75]

Following the Spanish Conquest of Mesoamerica, the Vice-royalty of New Spain (Virreinato de Nueva España), also known as "New Spain," was established. New Spain was a vice-royalty of the crown of Castile, of the Spanish empire, which comprised of territories in the north overseas 'Septentrion' (North America and Philippines).

Within this Septentrion included most of the United States west of the Mississippi River, including the lower gulf coast and all of Florida. Additionally, New Spain included the Caribbean, Mexico and all of Central America excluding Panama.

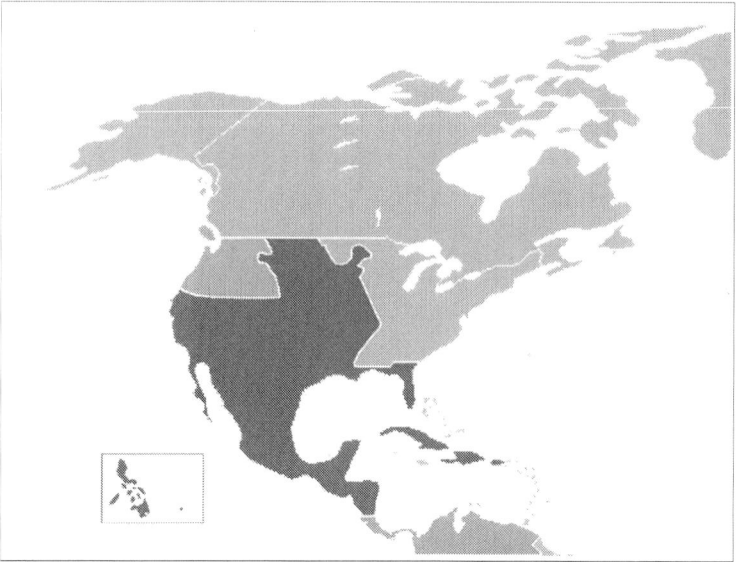

*Map of New Spain with territories claimed, although not all controlled.*[250]

The Viceroyalty of New Spain's territory included:

- The Bay Islands until 1643
- The Cayman Islands until 1670
- Central America to the southern border of Costa Rica until 1821
- Cuba to 1898
- Florida
- Hispaniola including Haiti until 1697
- Santo Domingo until 1821
- Jamaica until 1655
- Mariana Islands 1898
- Mexico until 1821
- Philippines 1898
- Puerto Rico 1898
- The Southwest United States
- British Columbia and Alaska, redefined by the Adams-Onís Treaty in 1819
- Venezuela until 1739

These territories were separated into provinces that were led by a governor whom was responsible for the province's administration and leading the province's army and local militias. The Spanish provinces were grouped together under five high courts that were called, "Audiencias" at Santo Domingo, Mexico City, Guatemala, Guadalajara and Manila. Both the high courts and the governors had autonomy from the Viceroy and carried out most of their duties on their own. Only on important issues did the Viceroy become involved in ruling the provinces directly.

As Spain's global power weakened, the previous colonies of what was once the Viceroyalty of New Spain, all eventually became independent nations of their own right. Their descendants, combined the cultures of the indigenous population and that of the European cultures that came and settled into their own cultures.

In it's height, the Maya civilization had one of the richest cultures in the New World. Today, there's an estimated 20 to 30 million direct descendants of the ancient Maya civilization that currently reside in southern Mexico, Belize, Honduras, El Salvador and Guatemala.

# References

1. Map of the Mayan Civilization cultural area by © Sémhur / Wikimedea Commons / CC-BY-SA-3.0 2. Martin & Grube 2000, p. 102. Sharer & Traxler 2006, p. 357.
2. Martin & Grube 2000, p. 102. Sharer & Traxler 2006, p. 357.
3. Sharer, Robert with Traxler, Loa. The Ancient Maya. p. 263.
4. Ortiz, P. & M. Del C. Rodriguez. 1999. Olmec ritual behavior at El Manati: a sacred space, in D.C. Grove & R.A. Joyce (ed.) Social Patterns in Pre-Classic Mesoamerica: 225-54. Washington (D.C.): Dumbarton Oaks.
5. Ortiz, P. & M. Del C. Rodriguez. 2000. The Sacred Hill of El Manati: A Preliminary Discussion of the Site's Ritual Paraphernalia, in J.E. Clark & M.E. Pye (ed.) Olmec Art and Archaeology in Mesoamerica (Studies in the History of Art 58): 75-93. Washington (D.C.): Center for Advanced Study in the Visual Arts, National Gallery of Art.
6. Love, M., D. Castillo, R. Ugarte, B. Damiata, & J. Steinberg. 2005. Investigaciones arqueologicas en el monticulo 1 de La Blanca, Costa Sur de Guatemala, in J.P. Laporte, B. Arroyo & H.E. Mejia (ed.) XVIII Simposio de Investigaciones Arqueologicas en Guatemala: 959-69. Guatemala City, Guatemala: Ministerio de Cultura y Deportes, Instituto de Antropologia e Historia, Asociacion Tikal, Foundation for the Advancement of Mesoamerican Studies, Inc.
7. Cyphers, A. 1993. Women, rituals, and social dynamics at ancient Chalcatzingo. Latin American Antiquity 4: 209-24.
8. Marcus, J. 1998. Women's Ritual in Formative Oaxaca: Figurine-making, Divination, Death, and the Ancestors. Memoirs 33. Ann Arbor:University of Michigan Museum of Anthropology.
9. Joyce, R.A. 2003. Making something of herself: embodiment in life and death at Playa de los Muertos, Honduras. Cambridge Archaeological Journal 13: 248-61.
10. Marcus, J. 1999. Men's and women's ritual in Formative

Oaxaca, in D.C. Grove & R.A. Joyce (ed.) Social Patterns in Pre-Classic Mesoamerica: 67-96. Washington (D.C.): Dumbarton Oaks.

11. GROVE, D.C. & S.D. GILLESPIE. 2002. Middle Formative domestic ritual at Chalcatzingo, Morelos, in E Plunker (ed.) Domestic Ritual in Ancient Mesoamerica. (Cotsen Institue of Archeology Monograph 46): 11-19. Los Angeles: Cotsen Institute of Archaeology at UCLA

12. Acemoglu, Robinson, Daron, James A. (2012). Why Nations Fail. p. 143 ISBN 978-0-397-71921-8

13. Mayan Stela, Copan, Honduras

14. Mayan Figurines, 600-900AD made in Jaina, Maya Area, Campeche, Mexico. photo: Bruce M. White courtesy Princeton University Art Museum.

15. The Mayan Long Count Calendar. Photo credit: Hannah Gleghorn.

16. Mayan Calendar Diagram by Centro de Estudios del Mundo Maya.

17. Tzolkin Day Signs and Names Diagram by Centro de Estudios del Mundo Maya.

18. The Story of Writing: Alphabets, Hieroglyphs & Pictograms by Andrew Robinson Credit: Photo by Columbia Pictures.

19. Liz Sonneborn (January 2007). Chronology of the American Indian History. Infobase Publishing. p. 3. Retrieved 29 November 2011.

20. Jennifer Viegas (November 2009) "First Americans Endured 20,000-Year Layover." Retrieved 2009-11-18. Page 2.

21. "Method and Theory in American Archaeology". Gordon Willey and Philip Phillips. University of Chicago. 1958. Retrieved 2009-11-20.

22. "Learn about Y-DNA Haplogroup Q" (Verbal tutorial possible). Wendy Tymchuk - Senior Technical Editor. Genebase Systems. 2008. Retrieved 2009-11-21.

23. Paleo-Indians hunting a glytodont. Heinrich Harder (1858–1935), c.1920.

24. Jacobs, James Q. (2001). "The Paleoamericans: Issues and Evidence relating to the Peopling of the New World". Retrieved 2006-07-24.

25. Jacobs, James Q. (2002). "Paleoamerican origins: A Review of Hypotheses and Evidence Relating to the Origins of the First Americans". Retrieved 2006-07-24.
26. Obsidian Projectile Point. R. Villalobos, Museo de Arquelogia de Guatemala, Puerta Parada, 9500 BC.
27. "Blame North America Megafauna Extinction On Climate Change, Not Human Ancestors". ScienceDaily. 2001.
28. Fiedel, Stuart J (1992). Prehistory of the Americas. Cambridge University Press.
29. Stuart B. Schwartz, Frank Salomon (1999-12-28). The Cambridge History of the Native Peoples of the Americas. Cambridge University Press.
30. Pielou, E.C. (1991). After the Ice Age : The Return of Life to Glaciated North America. University Of Chicago Press.
31. Atlatl weights and carved stone gorgets from Poverty Point. 2009-03-02 Heironymous Rowe CC-BY-SA-3.0; Released under GNU license.
32. Wm. Jack Hranicky; Wm Jack Hranicky Rpa (17 June 2010). North American Projectile Points - Revised. AuthorHouse. p. 135.
33. Vance T. Holliday (1997). Paleoindian geoarchaeology of the southern High Plains. University of Texas Press. p. 15.
34. The First Americans: In Pursuit of Archaeology's Greatest Mystery.. New York: Random House,. 2002. p. 14.
35. Wolfgang H. Berger; Elizabeth Noble Shor (25 April 2009).Ocean: reflections on a century of exploration. University of California Press. p. 397.
36. McHugh, Tom; Hobson, Victoria (1979). The Time of the Buffalo. University Of Nebraska Press.
37. Defrance, S. D.; Keefer, D. K.; Richardson, J. B.; Alvarez, A. n. U. (2010). "Late Paleo-Indian Coastal Foragers: Specialized Extractive". Susan D. deFrance, David K. Keefer, James B. Richardson and Adan Umire Alvarez (Society for American Archaeology) 12 (4): 413–426.
38. "Alberta History pre 1800". Jasper Alberta. 2009.
39. Bradley, B. and Stanford, D. "The North Atlantic ice-edge corridor: a possible Palaeolithic route to the New World." World Archaeology 34, 2004.

40. Lauber, Patricia. Who Came First? New Clues to Prehistoric Americans. Washington, D.C.: National Geographic Society, 2003.

41. "National Parks Service Southeastern Archaeological Center: The Paleoindian Period."

42. "Science News Online: Early New World Settlers Rise in East" Science News. 2000.

43. . National Historic Landmark summary listing. National Park Service.

44. "Monte Verde Archaeological Site - UNESCO World Heritage Centre".

45. "CNN.com: Man in Americas Earlier Than Thought". 2004-11-18.

46. Ignacio Villarreal (2010-08-25). "Mexican Archaeologists Extract 10,000 Year-Old Skeleton from Flooded Cave in Quintana Roo".

47. "Skull in Underwater Cave May Be Earliest Trace of First Americans - NatGeo News Watch". 2011-02-18.

48. "Does skull prove that the first Americans came from Europe?". The University of Texas at Austin - Web Central

49. Jordan, David K (2009). "Prehistoric Beringia". University of California-San Diego.

50. Bernal Díaz's Verdadera Historia de la Conquista de Nueva España ( The Conquest of New Spain ), pp.59–66.

51. The shoals are named as Los Alacranes ("the scorpions") by Bernal Díaz and Cervantes de Salazar, with Cervantes also calling them Las Viboras ("the vipers"). See Ch. XXII of Crónica de la Nueva España, and also The Valdivia Shipwreck (1511), which follows Cervantes

52. The landing place is around the "Rio Hondo" or possibly Cozumel or a little further to the south. See The Valdivia Shipwreck (1511) (1999).

53. Bernal Díaz uses the term Cacique, a word deriving from Caribbean languages such as Taíno and used by the Spanish generally for tribal chieftains; he also gives the word Calachiones as the local title. See The Conquest of New Spain, p.65.

54. Clendinnen, Inga; Ambivalent Conquests: Maya and

Spaniard in Yucatán, 1517-1570. (pgs 11-12).

55. The numbers for Grijalva's expedition are as given by Bernal Díaz, who participated in the voyage. See Díaz del Castillo (1963, p.27).

56. Guerrero is reported by Bernal Díaz to have responded, "Brother Aguilar, I am married and have three children, and they look on me as a Cacique here, and a captain in time of war....But my face is tattooed and my ears are pierced. What would the Spaniards say if they saw me like this? And look how handsome these children of mine are!" (p.60). However, other 16th-century sources say that Aguilar did not actually talk to Guerrero in person, but merely sent him a message (Gómara's version) or was unable to communicate with him at all (Cortés, de Landa), since if Guerrero was indeed near Chetumal that was some 400km from Cozumel. The quote attributed to Guerrero may well be a dramatic invention of Díaz. See discussion in Romero (1992, pp.7—10).

57. Later in the voyage a young woman, La Malinche, would be given to Cortés as a slave by the Chontal Maya inhabitants of the Tabasco coast. La Malinche spoke Nahuatl, the language of the Aztecs and a regional lingua franca, as well as Chontal Maya, which was also understood by Aguilar. Cortés used those two to communicate with the central Mexican peoples and the Aztec court. The Conquest of New Spain, pp.85–87.

58. Clendinnen, Inga; Ambivalent Conquests: Maya and Spaniard in Yucatan, (pg 23) 1517-1570.

59. Jones, Grant D. (1998). The Conquest of the Last Maya Kingdom. Stanford, California, USA: Stanford University Press

60. Feldman, Lawrence H. (2000). Lost Shores, Forgotten Peoples: Spanish Explorations of the South East Maya Lowlands. Durham, North Carolina, US: Duke University Press.

61. Lovell, W. George (2005). Conquest and Survival in Colonial Guatemala: A Historical Geography of the Cuchumatán Highlands, 1500–1821 (3rd ed.). Montreal, Canada: McGill-Queen's University Press.

62. Hardoy, Jorge E. (July 1991). "Antiguas y Nuevas Capitales Nacionales de América Latina". Revista EURE (Revista

Latinoamericana de Estudios Urbanos Regionales) (Santiago, Chile: Universidad Católica de Chile) XVII (52/53): 7–26.

63. Schwartz, Norman B. (1990). Forest Society: A Social History of Petén, Guatemala. Ethnohistory. Philadelphia, Pennsylvania, USA: University of Pennsylvania Press
64. Jones, Grant D. (2009). "The Kowoj in Ethnohistorical Perspective". In Prudence M. Rice and Don S. Rice (eds.). The Kowoj: identity, migration, and geopolitics in late postclassic Petén, Guatemala. Boulder, Colorado, US: The University Press Colorado. pp. 55–69.
65. Rice, Prudence M. and Don S. Rice (2009). "Introduction to the Kowoj and their Petén Neighbors". In Prudence M. Rice and Don S. Rice (eds.). The Kowoj: identity, migration, and geopolitics in late postclassic Petén, Guatemala. Boulder, Colorado, US: The University Press Colorado.
66. The 'macuahuitl': model displayed as part of the British Museum Moctezuma exhibition, London (bottom); artist's impression by Felipe Dávalos (top). Photos by Ian Mursell/Mexicolore.
67. Maya ruler, warrior, peasant levy Based on the Bonampak murals, a gold disc found on the Sacred Cenote in Chicen Itza and terracotta figurines from the island of Jaina. Source: Osprey Military Men-At-Arms series 101 "The Conquistadores" by Terence Wise. Illustrator: Angus McBride.
68. Means, Philip Ainsworth (1917). History of the Spanish Conquest of Yucatan and of the Itzas. Papers of the Peabody Museum of American Archaeology and Ethnology, Harvard University. VII. Cambridge, Massachussetts, USA: Peabody Museum of Archaeology and Ethnology.
69. Feldman, Lawrence H. (2000). Lost Shores, Forgotten Peoples: Spanish Explorations of the South East Maya Lowlands. Durham, North Carolina, US: Duke University Press.
70. Rice, Prudence M. (2009a). "The Archaeology of the Kowoj: Settlement and Architecture at Zacpetén". In Prudence M. Rice and Don S. Rice (eds.). The Kowoj: identity, migration, and geopolitics in late postclassic Petén, Guatemala. Boulder, Colorado, US: University Press of Colorado. pp. 81–83

71. Pugh, Timothy W. (2009). "Residential and Domestic Contexts at Zacpetén". In Prudence M. Rice and Don S. Rice (eds.). The Kowoj: identity, migration, and geopolitics in late postclassic Petén, Guatemala. Boulder, Colorado, US: University Press of Colorado. pp. 141–191.

72. Drawing accompanying text in Book XII of the 16th-century Florentine Codex (compiled 1540–1585), showing Nahuas of conquest-era central Mexico suffering from smallpox.

73. Chichen Itza at Spring Equinox photo by Shawn Christie. Chichen Itza at Spring Equinox during the equinox the sun casts its rays on the pyramid, forming seven isosceles triangles that resemble the body of a serpent 37 yards long slithering downwards until it joins the huge serpent's head carved in stone at the bottom of the stairway. It is said this snake is trying to make it to the well of sacrifice which is in the same direction. This photo was taken that day after the actual spring equinox. The day prior was cloudy and no serpent was seen. This photo was taken on March 22, 2010 in Chichén-Itzá, Yucatan, MX, using a Nikon D300.

74. Sculpture in the Temple of the Warriors, Chichén Itzá Yucatán, Mexico. Photo by Jeremy Woodhouse.

75. The Pyramid of Kukulcan seen from the Temple of the Warriors at Chichen-Itza.

76. Kaplan, Jonathan (2011) Conclusion: The Southern Maya Region and the Problem of Unities. In The Southern Maya in the Late Preclassic: The Rise and Fall of an Early Mesoamerican Civilization. Michael W. Love and Jonathan Kaplan, eds.; 490-532. University Press of Colorado, Boulder.

77. Kaplan, Jonathan (2008) Hydraulics, Cacao, and Complex Developments at Preclassic Chocolá, Guatemala: Evidence and Implications. Latin American Antiquity 19(4):399-413.

78. Herr, Sarah H. "The Latest Research on the Earliest Farmers." Archaeology Southwest. Vol. 23, No. 1, Winter 2009, p. 1

79. 1491: New Revelations of the Americas Before Columbus by Charles C. Mann, 2005.

80. Portion of the hieroglyphic Stairway with Maya glyphs at El Palmar. The fragmented block represents an emblem glyph of Kaan (Snake) dynasty at Calakmul, one of the most powerful

Ancient Maya dynasties. Photo by Kenichiro Tsukamoto.

81. The Meaning of Words: New Evidence of Ancient Maya History. by Fabio Esteban Amador of National Geographic Waitt Grants Program onApril 25, 2011.

82. Calakmul largest pyramid, referred to as Structure 2. Photo credit: Pete Fordham.

83. One of Three Scribes in Mural from Maya House 10K-2 at Xultun Photo by Tyrone Turner © 2012 National Geographic.

84. Maya warrior from set of History Channel's "Warriors: Maya Armegadon." Photo by Tom Mills, 2009.

85. Robert H. Fuson, ed., The Log of Christopher Columbus, Tab Books, 1992, International Marine Publishing.

86. Columbus (1991, p.87). Or "for with fifty men they can all be subjugated and made to do what is required of them." (Columbus & Toscanelli, 2010, p.41 ).

87. Bakewell, Peter. A History of Latin America. Blackwell Publishers, pp. 129–130.

88. The Doctrine of Discovery and the Christian Conquest of the World." By Nick Gier, Professor Emeritus, University of Idaho.

89. Collection des Mémoires sur l'Amérique, Recueil des Pièces sur le Mexique trad., par Ternaux-Compans, p. 307.

90. Salisbury, Stephen (2012-05-12). The Mayas, the Sources of Their History Dr. Le Plongeon in Yucatan, His Account of Discoveries.

91. Relation des choses de Yucatan. By Diego de Landa, Paris, 1864, pp. 44, 316.

92. Salisbury, Stephen (2012-05-12). The Mayas, the Sources of Their History Dr. Le Plongeon in Yucatan, His Account of Discoveries.

93. Relacion de las Cosas de Yucatan, de Diego de Landa. By L. Abbé Brasseur de Bourbourg. Paris, 1864, page 347.

94. Petén. Clay. height 14.8 cm Seated figure with removable helmet (Kohaw).

95. Aveni, Anthony F., Empires of Time, Tauris Parke Paperbacks, 2000.

96. Ruggles, Clive L.N., Ancient Astronomy, ABC-CLIO, 2005.

97. Anzovin, Steven et al., Famous First Facts International

Edition, H. W. Wilson Company (2000).

98. The Dresden Codex, pp. 47, 48, 50, 51, 52, first redrawing by Humboldt in 1810. Alexander von Humboldt: Vues des Cordillères et Monuments des Peuples Indigènes de l'Amérique. Paris, 1810, p. 416, Plate 45.

99. Teresi, Dick, Lost Discoveries: The Ancient Roots of Modern Science—from the Babylonians to the Maya, Simon and Schuster, 2002.

100. Nikolai Grube: Der Dresdner Maya-Kalender: Der vollständige Codex. Verlag Herder, Freiburg, 2012.

101. Sharer, Robert J.; with Loa P. Traxler (2006). The Ancient Maya (6th, fully revised ed.). Stanford, California: Stanford University Press.

102. Noguez, Xavier; Manuel Hermann Lejarazu ;Merideth Paxton and Henrique Vela (August 2009). "Códices Mayas [Maya codices]". Arqueología Mexicana: Códices prehispánicos y coloniales tempranos – Catálogo (Editorial Raíces) Special Edition (31): 10–23.

103. Ciudad Ruiz, Andrés; and Alfonso Lacadena (1999). J.P. Laporte and H.L. Escobedo. ed. "El Códice Tro-Cortesiano de Madrid en el contexto de la tradición escrita Maya [The Tro-Cortesianus Codex of Madrid in the context of the Maya writing tradition]" . Simposio de Investigaciones Arqueológicas en Guatemala, 1998 (Guatemala City, Guatemala: Museo Nacional de Arqueología y Etnología): 876–888.

104. Madrid Codex (replica) in the Museum of the Americas, Madrid. Late Postclassic Maya book. Simon Burchell 14 April 2012.

105. The Codex Perez; An Ancient Mayan Hieroglyphic Book, A photographic facsimile reproduced from the original in the Bibliothèque Nationale, Paris, by Theodore A. Willard. Glendale, California: The Arthur H. Clark Company, 1933.

106. Bruce Love "The Paris Codex." Austin: University of Texas Press. 1994.

107. Paris Codex, leaves 21-22 from Compendio Xcaret.

108. The pyramid in the Mayan city of Chichen Itza. Photograph: Steve Allen/Getty Images.

163

109. Early Civilizations in the Americas: Almanac. (2005). Gale Cengage.
110. Gibbard, P. and van Kolfschoten, T. (2004) "The Pleistocene and Holocene Epochs" Chapter 22. In Gradstein, F. M., Ogg, James G., and Smith, A. Gilbert (eds.), A Geologic Time Scale 2004 Cambridge University Press, Cambridge.
111. Field Museum (2008, February 28). Centuries-old Maya Blue Mystery Finally Solved. ScienceDaily.
112. A mural depicting ancient Maya heart extraction at Chichén Itzá in Mexico Bristol Museum. Photo Norman Hammond.
113. Aoyama, Kazuo (2005). "Classic Maya Warfare and Weapons spear, dart, and arrow points of Aguateca and Copan". Ancient Mesoamerica (Cambridge University Press) 16 (2): 291–304.
114. Barrett, Jason W.; and Andrew K. Scherer (2005). "Stones Bones and Crowded Plazas Evidence for Terminal Classic Maya warfare at Colha, Belize". Ancient Mesoamerica (Cambridge University Press) 16 (1): 101–18.
115. Vidal Lorenzo, Cristina; Juan Antonio Valdés and Gaspar Muñoz Cosme (2007). "El Clásico Terminal y el abandono de los palacios de La Blanca, Petén." XX Simposio de Investigaciones Arqueológicas en Guatemala, 2006 (edited by J.P. Laporte, B. Arroyo and H. Mejía). Museo Nacional de Arqueología y Etnología, Guatemala. pp. 561–576.
116. Vidal Lorenzo, Cristina; and Gaspar Muñoz Cosme (Undated). "Guatemala: La ciudad Maya de La Blanca". Madrid, Spain: Museo Nacional Centro de Arte Reina Sofía. pp. 45–50.
117. The ancient art of atlatl throwing by Wikipedia.
118. Atlatl throwing, Codex Becker, fol. 10. Graz, Austria, 1961.
119. Sanders, William and David Webster (1988) The Mesoamerican Urban Tradition. American Anthropologist 90(3): 521-546.
120. Howler monkey statue, temple 11, World Heritage Site of Copan (13 May 2009). Adalberto Hernandez Vega from Copan Ruinas, Honduras.
121. The Maize God as scribe. Francis Robicsek: The Maya Book of the Dead. The Ceramic Codex, University of Virginia Art

Museum (1981).

122. Foster, Lynn V. (2001) Handbook to Life in the Ancient Maya World. New York: Facts on File, Inc..

123. Bunson, Margaret R., and Stephen M. Bunson. (1996) Warfare, Maya. Encyclopedia of Ancient Mesoamerica. New York: Facts On File, Inc., 1996.

124. Barrett, Jason and Andrew Scherer. (2005) Stones, Bones, and Crowded Plazas: Evidence for Terminal Classic Maya Warfare at Colha, Belize. Ancient Mesoamerica 16(1): 101-118.

125. S.W. Miles, The Sixteenth-Century Pokom-Maya. The American Philosophical Society, Philadelphia 1957. pg 749, quoting Fuentes y Guzmán and Las Casas.

126. Evon Z. Vogt, Tortillas for the Gods. A Symbolic Analysis of Zinacanteco Rituals. Harvard University Press, Cambridge 1976.

127. Barbara Tedlock, Time and the Highland Maya. University of New Mexico Pres, Albuquerque 1992.

128. Ralph L. Roys, The Book of Chilam Balam of Chumayel. University of Oklahoma Press, Norman 1967.

129. Bruce Love, 'Yucatec Sacred Breads Through Time'. In William F. Hanks and Don Rice, Word and Image in Maya Culture. Salt Lake City: University of Utah Press 1989.

130. Thompson, J. Eric S. (1970). Maya History and Religion. Civilization of the American Indian Series, No. 99. Norman: University of Oklahoma Press.

131. Alfred M. Tozzer, Landa's Relación de las cosas de Yucatán. A Translation. Peabody Museum, Cambridge MA 1941.

132. Alfred M. Tozzer, A Comparative Study of the Mayas and the Lacandones. Archaeological Institute of America. The Macmillan Company, New York 1907.

133. Accession: see Piedras Negras stela 11; illness and burial: Las Casas, in Miles 1957: 750, 773; drought: Landa, in Tozzer 1941: 54, 180-181.

134. David Joralemon, 'Ritual Blood Sacrifice Among the Ancient Maya: Part I', in Primera Mesa Redonda de Palenque Part II, pp. 59–75. The Robert Louis Stevenson School, Pre-Columbian Art Research, Pebble Beach 1974.

135. Joyce, Rosemary; Richard Edging; Karl Lorenz and Susan

Gillespie (1991). "Olmec Bloodletting: An Iconographic Study". In V M Fields. Sixth Palenque Round Table 1986. Norman, Oklahoma, USA.: University of Oklahoma Press.

136. Bancroft, Hubert Howe (1882). The Native Races, Volume 2, Civilized Nations.

137. Joralemon, D. (1974). "Ritual Blood-Sacrifice among the Ancient Maya: Part I". In Merle Green Robertson (ed.). Primera Mesa Redonda de Palenque. Pebble Beach, California, USA: Robert Louis Stevenson School, Pre-Columbian Art Research. pp. 59–76.

138. De Landa, Diego (1937). Yucatan Before and After the Conquest: An English translation by William Gates of Relation des choses de Yucatan de Diego de Landa.

139. Montero Lopez, Coral (July 2009). "Sacrifice and feasting among the classic Maya elite, and the importance of the white-tailed deer: is there a regional pattern?". Journal of Historical and European Studies (Bundoora, Victoria, Australia: School of Historical and European Studies, La Trobe University) 2: 53–68.

140. Marcus, Joyce (October 1978). "Archaeology and Religion: A Comparison of the Zapotec and Maya". World Archaeology (Abingdon, UK.: Routledge Journals) 10 (2): 172–191.

141. Tiesler, Vera; Andrea Cucina (December 2006). "Procedures in Human Heart Extraction and Ritual Meaning: A Taphonomic Assessment of Anthropogenic Marks in Classic Maya Skeletons". Latin American Antiquity 17 (4): 493–510.

142. de Anda Alanís, Guillermo (2007). "Sacrifice and Ritual Body Mutilation in Postclassical Maya Society: Taphonomy of the Human Remains from Chichén Itzá's Cenote Sagrado". In Vera Tiesler and Andrea Cucina (eds.). New Perspectives on Human Sacrifice and Ritual Body Treatments in Ancient Maya Society. Interdisciplinary Contributions to Archaeology. Michael Jochim (series ed.). New York, USA.: Springer Verlag. pp. 190–208.

143. Baudez, Claude F.; and Peter Matthews (1978 or 1979). "Capture and sacrifice at Palenque". In Merle Greene Robertson and Donnan Call Jeffers. Tercera Mesa Redonda de Palenque. IV.

144. Stuart, David (2003). "La ideología del sacrificio entre los mayas". Arqueología mexicana (Mexico City.: Editorial Raíces) XI (63): 24–29.

145. Pendergast, David M. (1988). "Lamanai Stela 9: The Archaeological Context". Research Reports on Ancient Maya Writings 20. Washington DC, USA.: Centre for Maya Research.

146. Marí, Carlos (27 December 2005). "Evidencian sacrificios humanos en Comalcaco: Hallan entierro de menores mayas". Reforma.

147. Eppich, Keith (2009). "Feast and Sacrifice at El Perú-Waka': The N14-2 Deposit as Dedication". The PARI Journal X (2).

148. Lee, J.C. (1996). The Amphibians and Reptiles of the Yucatan Peninsula. New York, USA.: Cornell University.

149. Reilly, F.Kent (1991). "Olmec iconographic influences on symbols of Maya rulership". Sixth Palenque Round Table 1986. Norman, Oklahoma, USA.: University of Oklahoma Press.

150. Berryman, Carrie Anne. (2007) "Captive Sacrifice and Trophy Taking Among the Ancient Maya" in The Taking and Displaying of Human Body Parts By Amerindians, edited by Richard J Chacon & David H Dye, pp. 377-399. Chapter 13. Springer Science + Business Media, New York.

151. McAnany, A. Patricia (1998). "Ancestors and the Classic Maya Built Environme."

152. O'Mansky, Matt & Arthur A Demarest. (2007) "Status Rivalry and Warfare in the Development and Collapse of Classic Maya Civilization" in Latin American Indigenous Warfare and Ritual Violence, edited by Richard J Chacon & Ruben G Mendoza, pp. 11-34. Chapter 1. The University of Arizona Press, Tucson.

153. Spence, W. Michael; Christine D. White, Fred J. Longstaffe, and Kimberly R. Law (2004). Human Trophies Worn by the Sacrificial Soldiers from the Feathered Serpent Pyramid, Teotihuacan. New York: Cambridge University Press.

154. Casas. "Apologética Historia Sumaria." 1967: 504-505

155. López Austin, Alfredo; and Leonardo López Luján (1999). Mito y realidad de Zuyuá: Serpiente emplumada y las

transformaciones mesoamericanas del clásico al posclásico. Mexico: COLMEX & FCE. ISBN 968-16-5889-2.

156. Teotihuacan - Temple of the Feathered Serpent. 14 April 2008. Wikimedia Commons.

157. Allen J. Christenson, Art and Sociey in a Highland Maya Community: The Altarpiece of Santiago Atitlán. Austin: University of Texas Press. 2001.

158. Rafael Girard, Los Chortis ante el problema maya. Guatemala: Editorial Cultura. 1949.

159. Barbara Tedlock, Time and the Highland Maya. University of New Mexico Pres, Albuquerque 1992.

160. David Stuart, The Order of Days. Harmony Books, New York 2011.

161. Orellana, Sandra L. (Spring 1981). "Idols and Idolatry in Highland Guatemala". Ethnohistory (Duke University Press) 28 (2): 157–177.

162. David Stuart, The Inscriptions from Temple XIX at Palenque. San Francisco: The Pre-Columbian Art Research Institute 2005.

163. Michael D. Coe, 'A Model of Ancient Maya Community Structure in the Maya Lowlands', Southwestern Journal of Anthropology 21 (1965).

164. Linda A. Brown, 'Planting the Bones: Hunting Ceremonialism at Contemporary and Nineteenth-Century Shrines in the Guatemalan Highlands', Latin American Antiquity 16(2): 131-146 (2005).

165. Victor Montejo, El Kanil, Man of Lightning. Signal Books, Carrboro N.C. 1984.

166. Francisco de Fuentes y Guzmán, Recordación Florida. 2 vols. Madrid: Atlas. 1969.

167. Takeshi Inomata, 'Plazas, Performers, and Spectators'. Current Anthropology 47 (5), 2006.

168. Martin, Simon, and Nikolai Grube, Chronicle of Maya Kings and Queens. Thames&Hudson 2000.

169. Nikolai Grube and Werner Nahm, 'A Census of Xibalba', in Maya Vase Books Vol. 4, New York 1994. Kerr Associates.

170. J.E.S. Thompson, Maya Hieroglyphic Writing. University of Oklahoma Press, Norman 1960. pg 71, quoting Nuñez de la

Vega.

171. Robert S. Carlson, and Martin Prechtel, 'The Flowering of the Dead: An Interpretation of Highland Maya Culture'. Man 26-1 (1991): 22-42.

172. Calixta Guiteras Holmes, Perils of the Soul. The World View of a Tzotzil Indian. New York: The Free Press of Glencoe. 1961.

173. Kerry Hull, 'The Grand Ch'orti' Epic: The Story of the Kumix Angel'. Acta Mesoamericana 20 (2009): 131-140.

174. The Hero Twins shooting a perched bird demon with a blowgun. Izapa Stela 25. Drawing of Izapa Stela 25 taken from Japanese Wikipedia. 20 February 2006.

175. Gabrielle Vail, 'Pre-Hispanic Maya Religion. Conceptions of divinity in the Postclassic Maya codices'. Ancient Mesoamerica 11(2000): 123-147.

176. Scholes, France V., and Ralph L. Roys, The Maya Chontal Indians of Acalan-Tixchel. University of Oklahoma Press, Norman 1968.

177. Sarah C. Blaffer, The Black-man of Zinacantan. University of Texas Press, Austin 1972.

178. Boremanse, Didier, Contes et mythologie des indiens lacandons. Paris: L'Harmattan. 1986. (Also in Spanish: Cuentos y mitología de los lacandones. Tradición oral maya. Editorial: Academia de Geografia e Historia de Guatemala.).

179. Lauren Landry (December 11th, 2012). "Boston University Professor Reminds Us: The Mayan Calendar Doesn't Say the World Will End". BostInno.

180. Bierhorst, John (ed.), The Monkey's Haircut and Other Stories Told by the Maya. New York: William Morrow 1986.

181. Nicholson, Irene, Mexican and Central American Mythology. London: Paul Hamlyn. 1967.

182. Danien, Elin C., Maya Folktales from the Alta Verapaz. University of Pennsylvania, Museum of Archaeology and Anthropology, Philadelphia 2004.

183. Bierhorst,John, The Mythology of Mexico and Central America. Oxford U.P. 2002.

184. Roys, Ralph L. (translator), The Book of Chilam Balam of Chumayel. Norman: University of Oklahoma Press, 1967

169

[1933].

185. Copy of the Book of Chilam Balam of Ixil in the National Museum of Anthropology, Mexico City. 8 July 2008.

186. Paxton, Merideth (2001). 'Books of Chilam Balam', in: Oxford Encyclopedia of Mesoamerican Cultures Vol. 1. Oxford: Oxford University Press.

187. Knowlton, Timothy (2010). Maya Creation Myths: Words and Worlds of the Chilam Balam. Boulder: University Press of Colorado.

188. Christenson, Allen J. (trans.), ed. Popol Vuh: Literal Poetic Version: Translation and Transcription. Norman: University of Oklahoma Press. 2004.

189. Goetz, Delia, and Morley, Sylvanus Griswold, ed. Popol Vuh: The Sacred Book of the Ancient Quiché Maya By Adrián Recinos (1st ed.). Norman: University of Oklahoma Press. 1950.

190. The oldest written account of Popol Vuh. 1701 AD by Francisco Ximénez. Primera página del manuscrito del Popol Vuh, guardado en la Biblioteca de Newberry, Chicago, Colección Ayer. Wikimedia Commons. 17 April 2012.

191. Roys, Ralph L., Ritual of the Bacabs, University of Oklahoma Press. 1965.

192. Thompson, J. Eric S., Maya History and Religion, University of Oklahoma Press. 1970.

193. Table showing first 20 Maya numbers and their Arabic equivalents. Centro de Estudios del Mundo Maya. Yucatan, Mexico. Maya World Studies Center.

194. Freidel, David; and Linda Schele and Joy Parker (1993). Maya Cosmos: Three thousand years on the shaman's path. New York: William Morrow. ISBN [[Special:BookSources/0-88810-081-5|0-88810-081-5]]. OCLC 27430287.

195. Thompson, J. Eric S. (1929). "Maya Chronology: Glyph G of the Lunar Series". American Anthropologist, New Series 31 (2): pp.223–231. doi:10.1525/aa.1929.31.2.02a00010. ISSN 0002-7294. OCLC 51205515.

196. Thompson, J. Eric S. (1971). Maya Hieroglyphic Writing, an Introduction. 3rd edition. Norman.

197. "Clarifications: The Correlation Debate." Excerpt from

Tzolkin: Visionary Perspectives and Calendar Studies (Borderlands Science and Research Foundation, 1994, pages 31-36):

198. John Major Jenkins. "Tzolkin: Visionary Perspectives and Calendar Studies." Borderland Sciences Research Foundation; First Printing edition (1994). ISBN-10: 0945685165.

199. "Maya." Dictionary.com Unabridged. Random House, Inc. 19 Jan. 2013.

200. Picture of Temple I in Tikal, Guatemala, taken by Bruno Girin. (2005).

201. Sharer, Robert J.; with Loa P. Traxler (2006). The Ancient Maya (6th (fully revised) ed.). Stanford, CA: Stanford University Press. ISBN 0-8047-4817-9. OCLC 57577446.

202. The Mayan ruins of Copan Ruinas located near Copan, Honduras. Photograph by Kyle Hammons. July 14, 2009.

203. Hypothesized map of human migration based on mitochondrial DNA. Illustration by Mauricio Lucioni. 8 April 2010.

204. Paleoindian Point Types. "The Taking Of South America In Atlantean Times." frontiers-of-anthropology.blogspot.com. February 10, 2112.

205. John F. Hoffecker, Scott A. Elias. "Human Ecology of Beringia." June 2007. ISBN: 978-0-231-13060-8.

206. Bering Land Bridge. Survey of Meteorology. Thomson Higher Education. 2007.

207. Map: "The Bering Strait Land Bridge and the Migration of Early Indians" By Jose Arredondo, University of California Los Angeles.

208. Jennifer Viegas. "First Americans Endured 20,000-Year Layover." Discovery News. Feb. 13, 2008.

209. Kitchen A, Miyamoto MM, Mulligan CJ (2008) A Three-Stage Colonization Model for the Peopling of the Americas. PLoS ONE 3(2): e1596. doi:10.1371/journal.pone.0001596.

210. Mulligan CJ, Kitchen A, Miyamoto MM (2008) Updated Three-Stage Model for the Peopling of the Americas. PLoS ONE 3(9): e3199. doi:10.1371/journal.pone.0003199.

211. Maps depicting each phase of our three-step colonization model for the peopling of the Americas. From figure 4.

171

Kitchen A, Miyamoto MM, Mulligan CJ (2008) A Three-Stage Colonization Model for the Peopling of the Americas. PLoS ONE 3(2): e1596. doi:10.1371/journal.pone.0001596.

212. Inga Clendinnen. "Ambivalent Conquests: Maya and Spaniard in Yucatan, 1517-1570." Cambridge University Press. Apr 28, 2003.

213. Lidded effigy container in the form of a diving god ca. A.D. 1500. Late Postclassic Maya. Princeton University Art Museum.

214. Paleo-Indians butchering a bison at the end of the Ice Age with woolly mammoths looking on. Painting on exhibit at the Pembina State Museum, courtesy of the State Historical Society of North Dakota.

215. E.C. Pielou, After the Ice Age: The Return of Life to Glaciated North America (Chicago: University of Chicago Press) 1991:19 and note.

216. Gordon R. Willey and Philip Phillips (1957). Method and Theory in American Archaeology. University of Chicago Press. ISBN 978-0-226-89888-9.

217. "Archaic Period, Southeast Archaeological Center". Archived from the original on 5 December 2004.

218. Joe W. Saunders, Rolfe D. Mandel, Roger T. Saucier, E. Thurman Allen, C. T. Hallmark, Jay K. Johnson, Edwin H. Jackson, Charles M. Allen, Gary L. Stringer, Douglas S. Frink, James K. Feathers, Stephen Williams, Kristen J. Gremillion, Malcolm F. Vidrine, and Reca Jones, "A Mound Complex in Louisiana at 5400-5000 Years Before the Present", Science, 19 September 1997: Vol. 277 no. 5333, pp. 1796-1799.

219. Milanich, Jerald T. (1994). Archaeology of Precolumbian Florida. Gainesville, Florida: The University Press of Florida.

220. Michael Russo. "Archaic Shell Rings of the Southeast U.S." Southeast Archeological Center, National Park Service, Tallahassee. April 2006.

221. Archaic: 5500 to 500 B.C.- Overview. Crow Canyon Archaeological Center. 2011.

222. Time-Life Book Editors. (1993) The First Americans. Alexandria, Virginia: Time-Life Books. pp. 29, 30. ISBN 0-8094-9400-0.

223. Archaic camp scene by Martin Pate (Courtesy, Southeast Archeological Center, National Park Service).
224. Circa 5000 BC. Life-size mural by Greg Harlin.
225. Copan Stela B, dates to 731. One of the Great Kings: 18 Rabbits. Honduras. January 9, 2004.
226. An illustration showing Mayans playing the sacred ball game. .theancientweb.org.
227. Maya logogram of calendric Tzolkin Day20:Ajaw. Image created by CJLL Wright.
228. Lockhart, James (2001). Nahuatl as Written: Lessons in Older Written Nahuatl, with Copious Examples and Texts. UCLA Latin American studies, vol. 88; Nahuatl studies series, no. 6. Stanford and Los Angeles: Stanford University Press and UCLA Latin American Center Publications. ISBN 0-8047-4282-0. OCLC 46858459.
229. Schroeder, Susan (2007). "The Annals of Chimalpahin". In James Lockhart, Lisa Sousa, and Stephanie Wood (eds.). Sources and Methods for the Study of Postconquest Mesoamerican Ethnohistory (Provisional version ed.). Eugene: University of Oregon Wired Humanities Project. Retrieved 2008-05-16.
230. Schroeder, Susan (1991). Chimalpahin and the Kingdoms of Chalco. Tucson: University of Arizona Press. ISBN 0-8165-1182-9. OCLC 21976206.
231. Nahuatl dictionary (1997). Wired humanities project.
232. Coe, Michael D. "The Maya scribe and his World." Grolier Club (1973). ISBN: 978-0813905686.
233. HM 626: Kneeling Warrior with Shield. 600-900 AD, Mexico. Palmer Collection.
234. The Ball Court at Copán, Honduras. by Tatiana Proskouriakoff. Peabody Museum of Archaeology and Ethnology, Harvard College.
235. Map of Settlement area of Ancient Maya. Nepenthes, 18 July 2006.
236. Map of North America showing the extent of Late Pleistocene glaciation. Modified after Pielou, 1991.
237. Walker, M., S. Johnsen, S.O. Rasmussen, T. Popp, J.-P. Steffensen, P. Gibbard, W. Hoek, J. Lowe, A. John, B. John, S. Björck, L.C. Cwynar, K. Hughen, K. Konrad, K. Peter, B.

Kromer, T. Litt, D.J. Lowe, T. Nakagawa, R. Newnham, and J. Schwander (2008) Formal definition and dating of the GSSP (Global Stratotype Section and Point) for the base of the Holocene using the Greenland NGRIP ice core, and selected auxiliary records. Journal of Quaternary Science. 24(1):3–17.

238. Columbian mammoths were larger than mastodons. Both once roamed North America. (Velizar Simeonovski / The Field Museum, Chicago). Smithsonian magazine, April 2010.

239. San Lorenzo Monument 3 (also known as Colossal Head 3). Height: 178 cm. Museo de Antropología de Xalapa, Veracruz, Mexico. Photo by Maribel Ponce Ixba. 16 November 2006.

240. Burnett, R. L., Terry, R. E., Sweetwood, R. V., Webster, D., Murtha, T., & Silverstein, J.. Upland and Lowland Soil Resources of the Ancient Maya at Tikal, Guatemala. Soil Sci. Soc. Am. J.. 2012 76: 2083–2096.

241. Vernon L. Scarborough, Nicholas P. Dunning, Kenneth B. Tankersley, Christopher Carr, Eric Weaver, Liwy Grazioso, Brian Lane, John G. Jones, Palma Buttles, Fred Valdez, and David L. Lentz. "Water and sustainable land use at the ancient tropical city of Tikal, Guatemala". PNAS 2012.

242. "Classic Period collapse of the Central Maya Lowlands: Insights about human-environment relationships for sustainability". B. L. Turner and J. A. Sabloff. Proceedings of the National Academy of Sciences (2012) 109: 13908.

243. These are veneer stones of the dam identified by the UC researchers. What was once thought to be a sluice is outlined in red and is now filled with slump-down debris [Photo and Research Credit: University of Cincinnati researchers]. 2012.

244. "Development and Disintegration of Maya Political Systems in Response to Climate Change". Douglas J. Kennett, Sebastian F. M. Breitenbach, Valorie V. Aquino, Yemane Asmerom, Jaime Awe, James U.L. Baldini, Patrick Bartlein, Brendan J. Culleton, Claire Ebert, Christopher Jazwa, Martha J. Macri, Norbert Marwan, Victor Polyak, Keith M. Prufer, Harriet E. Ridley, Harald Sodemann, Bruce Winterhalder, and Gerald H. Haug. Science 9 November 2012: 338 (6108), 788-791. [DOI:10.1126/science.1226299].

245. William L. Merrill, Robert J. Hard, Jonathan B. Mabry, Gayle J. Fritz, Karen R. Adams, John R. Roney, and A. C.

MacWilliams . "The diffusion of maize to the southwestern United States and its impact". PNAS 2009.

246. A map of the southern-most area of Mesoamerica, showing important Formative Period sites. February 2008.

247. Illustration: Mirador Basin. "El Mirador, the Lost City of the Maya." Smithsonian magazine, May 2011.

248. Map of Preclassic Maya sites. Latin American Studies. Maya Maps. 2013.

249. Map of Maya Trade Routes. Latin American Studies. Maya Maps. 2013.

250. Map of New Spain in red, with territories claimed but not controlled in orange. Map of Viceroyalty of New Spain / Mapa del Virreinato de la Nueva España (siglo XVIII).

251. Georges Ifrah, "From One to Zero, a Universal History of Numbers", Penguin Books, 1987.

252. Hernan Garcia, Antonio Sierra, Gilberto Balam, Jeff Conant, and Hilberto Balam. "Wind in the Blood: Mayan Healing & Chinese Medicine." 1999.

253. G Ifrah, A universal history of numbers : From prehistory to the invention of the computer (London, 1998).

254. J B Lambert, B Ownbey-McLaughlin, and C D McLaughlin, Maya arithmetic, Amer. Sci. 68 (3) (1980), 249-255.

255. Lounsbury, Floyd G. Maya Numeration, Computation, and Calendrical Astronomy. In Dictionary Of Scientific Biography. New York, New York. Charles Scribner's Sons. Volume 15, Supplement 1. 1978. P. 759-818.

256. Visual explanation of a binary clock. Alexander Jones & Eric Pierce. 14 October 2006.

257. David Esparza Hidalgo, Nepohualtzintzin. Computador Prehispanico en Vigencia [The Nepohualtzintzin: a pre-Hispanic computer in use] (Mexico City, Mexico: Editorial Diana, 1977).

258. Bancroft, Hubert Howe (1882). "The Native Races, Volume 2, Civilized Nations. The works of Hubert Howe Bancroft", Volume 2. 1832-1918.

259. "The Maya Mathematical System." Authentic Maya. 2005.

260. Hooker, Richard. "Native American Creation Stories". Washington State University.

261. Walker, Amélie A. "My Trip to Xibalba and Back". Archaeological Institute of America. June 2000.

262. Mizrach, Steve. "The Mayan Sacbe System Analyzed as an Information Web". Florida International University.

263. Dennis Tedlock. "Popol Vuh: The Mayan Book of the Dawn of Life." 1996.

264. "It is believed that there is a supermassive black hole at the Galactic Center of the Milky Way." Credit: ESO. "Mysterious Flares Emitting From Sagittarius A." 9 February, 2012.

265. Lynn V. Foster. "Handbook to Life in the Ancient Maya World." July 7, 2005.

266. Photos of Maya men in traditional costume and figurine. Southwest Missouri State University. John Chuchiak. 2013.

267. "Popol Vuh : The Mayan Book of the Dawn of Life." Dennis Tedlock (Translator) 1996. edited by Jeeni Criscenzo 1997.

268. Justin Kerr. "Enchantment in Mesoamerica." Wall Street Journal. Dow Jones and Company, Inc.. Mar 26, 2011.

269. "The Pleiades, also known as the Seven Sisters" ESO/S. Brunier. eso.org. Photograph: b11. 3 December 2009.

270. Photograph of Stela C, Quirigua. Source: latinamericanstudies.org.

271. "The Sacred Tree of the Ancient Maya." Allen J. Christenson. Journal of Book of Mormon Studies: Volume - 6, Issue - 1, Pages: 1–23 Provo, Utah: Maxwell Institute, 1997.

272. Calabash tree, *Crescentia cujete*. Also known as: higuera tree. Description: This evergreen tropical tree grows up to 10 meters. It has rough bark, simple leaves, and greenish-yellow cauliflorous flowers. Its large spherical fruits have a hard green woody shell. Source: The Natural History Museum. 2013.

273. Friedel, David and Linda Schele, A Forest of Kings: the Untold Story of the Ancient Maya, Harper Perennial 1992.

274. Clare Green. "Pok ta Pok; The Mayan Ball Game. Athletes or Worshipers?" Chichen Itza. Jul 15, 2009.

275. The ball in front of the goal during a game of pok-ta-pok. Photo by Sputnik. Wikipedia. 14 May 2006.

276. Mary Miller. "Extreme Makeover: How painted bodies, flattened foreheads, and filed teeth made the Maya beautiful."

Archaeology Magazine, Volume 62 Number 1,
January/February 2009.

277. Photo  Courtesy: Vera Tiesler/Dirección de Antropología
Física. Archaeology Magazine, Volume 62 Number 1,
January/February 2009.

278. Photo Courtesy: Vera Tiesler. Archaeology Magazine, Volume
62 Number 1, January/February 2009.

279. Site at Ceibal dating to around 1000 BC. Photo Credit: Takeshi
Inomata. "Maya Civilization More Ancient Than Previously
Thought." Archaeology Magazine. April 26, 2013.

280. Kukulkan at its finest during the spring equinox. Chichen
Itza equinox March 2009. The famous decent of the snake at
the temple. Wikipedia. 21 March 2009.

281. Foster, Lynn V. "Handbook to Life in the Ancient Mayan
World." New York: Facts on File. 2002.

282. Schele, Linda, and David Freidel. "A Forest of Kings: The
Untold Story of the Ancient Maya." New York: Harper
Perennial. 1990.

283. Terry Rugeley, "Yucatan's Maya Peasantry and the Origins of
the Caste War." San Antonio. 1996.

284.  Jacinto Pac to Edward Rhys and John Kingdom, 18 February
1848 in Terry Rugeley, ed. and trans. Maya Wars:
Ethnographic Accounts from Nineteenth Century Yucatan,
(Norman, 2001).

285. Cecilio Chi to John Fancourt, 23 April 1849, in Rugeley, Maya
Wars.

286. Diorama made by the team at Te Mahi of Aztec chinampas at
the Museum of New Zealand Te Papa Tongarewa.

# Other books:

### The Maya : The Story of a People
by Njord Kane

### The Vikings : The Story of a People
by Njord Kane

### History of the Norse
by Njord Kane

### The Viking Stone Age : Birth of the Axe Culture
by Njord Kane

### Maya Math Simplified
by Njord Kane

.

19823192R00109

Printed in Great Britain
by Amazon